ICT in the Early Years

KT-165-282

London: Continuum,
2004

0826466443

GC 104175   GRIMSBY COLLEGE

LOCATION HG

WITHDRAWN 338

ACC. No. 104175

Other Classmates:

ICT in the Early Years

Mark O'Hara

GRIMSBY INSTITUTE OF
LIBRARIES
FURTHER & HIGHER EDUCATION

continuum

LONDON • NEW YORK

Continuum

The Tower Building
11 York Road
London SE1 7NX

15 East 26th Street
New York
NY 10010

www.continuumbooks.com

© Mark O'Hara 2004

All rights reserved. No part of this publication may be reproduced or
transmitted in any form or by any means, electronic or mechanical,
including photocopying, recording, or any information storage or
retrieval system, without prior permission in writing from the
publishers.

British Library Cataloguing-in-Publication Data
A catalogue record for this book is available from the British Library.

ISBN: 0–8264–6644–3 (paperback)

Typeset by BookEns Ltd, Royston, Herts.
Printed and bound in Great Britain by
Antony Rowe Ltd, Chippenham, Wiltshire

Contents

Contents

Acknowledgements

I would like to thank nursery and reception colleagues for their help in compiling the examples contained in the book and the enthusiasm they showed in looking for ways to incorporate ICT into their existing provision. I would also like to thank Dr Ros Garrick at Sheffield Hallam University for her valuable comments on the topic of ICT in the early years.

Preface

This book is about the use of Information and Communications Technology (ICT) in the early years of education. Computers (PCs) are one example of this, but in education ICT can be seen to encompass a wide range of technologies including telephones, fax machines, televisions, video, audio recorders, CD players, CD-ROMs, personal organisers, programmable and remote-operated toys and radios as well as computers. The examples used in the book reflect this diversity.

The book is also premised on the idea that the pedagogical knowledge and understanding possessed by good early years practitioners is every bit as important as technical *know how*. In other words, the best way for practitioners to make effective use of ICT is to base their practice on their existing expertise. Understanding young children as learners, understanding the role of the adult, and knowing how to establish stimulating learning environments are just as important as technological awareness and capability.

Introduction

ICT has become an increasingly prevalent feature in many aspects of life in contemporary western societies, including education. Children growing up in these societies are likely to spend large amounts of time watching television and videos, many will have access to home computers, and all will encounter a wide range of technology in their day-to-day lives (Edgington 1998). Within the field of early years education attitudes towards ICT can vary considerably. At one end of the continuum are advocates of its increasing use on the basis of hoped for socio-economic benefits (DfEE 1997b; DfES 2001). For others ICT is seen as a potentially useful tool but the prime criterion for judging its worth is *developmental appropriateness* and not socio-economic relevance (NAEYC 1996). ICT is not merely an end, but also a means to an end (Pierce 1994). At the other end of the continuum are those who see ICT as wholly inappropriate in early years settings, producing an impoverished educational experience for young children and threatening future health and social problems through over use (Oppenheimer 1997; McVeigh and Paton Walsh 2000). In part some of the concerns around ICT may stem from narrow definitions of the kind alluded to in the Preface about what is involved. While the term ICT may be used, when examples are offered they frequently centre on the use of computers, suggesting that the wider *communications* aspect is being omitted or overlooked.

The book begins with a short outline of some of the policy developments associated with the introduction of ICT into mainstream education settings in England and Wales since the establishment of the National Curriculum (DES 1989) and the Curriculum guidance for the foundation stage (QCA 2000). It goes on to raise some questions about possible gaps between policy rhetoric and the day-to-day reality in early years settings. The book then gives some examples of practice in nursery (age 3–4) and reception (age 4–5) classes. It draws on these examples as well as references to the literature on children as learners, early learning environments, and the role of the early years practitioner to make suggestions about teaching and learning involving ICT in early years education. Although the settings referred to are in the state sector and of necessity English, the subsequent discussion is intended to be of interest to early years practitioners anywhere who are using, or are considering using, ICT with their children.

1

The Drive to Include ICT in Early Years Practice

Policy developments, curriculum design and resourcing

In England and Wales positive statements in favour of the place of ICT in education can be found in numerous publications since the introduction of the National Curriculum in 1989 and before (DES 1989; NCC 1990; DfEE 1997a; BECTA 2000; Siraj-Blatchford and Siraj-Blatchford 2002). In some of these publications the inclusion of ICT in the curriculum is seen as helping to prepare children to participate fully in a world that is expected to continue changing rapidly as a result of the introduction of new information technologies (DfEE 1997b; QCA 1999). Such rationales frequently point to the inevitable advance of globalization and the need to maintain, and preferably enhance, the nation's economic position relative to other countries. Introducing ICT into the curriculum will ensure that children become more knowledgeable about information, become increasingly comfort-able with new technologies and are better able to exploit their potential (DfEE 1997b; DTI/DfEE 2001; DfES 2001).

> We need to build up the store of knowledge and keep abreast of rapid technological development if we are to prepare the future generation. (DfEE 1997c)

At the policy-making level there appears to be considerable common ground between England and Wales, the United States (Alliance for Childhood 2000) and many European countries in terms of the economic rationales offered in support of ICT in education, and in the types of policy initiatives being implemented (Commission of the European Communities 2001). At the time of writing, for example, all European Union (EU) member states possess official documentation intended to promote and enhance the use of ICT in schools supported by national projects. ICT learning objectives are contained in many European primary curricula, and while ICT is compulsory in initial teacher education (ITE) in only half of European states, all countries have in-service training programmes for serving practitioners. As in England and Wales, the EU documentation suggests that ICT is a clear priority area, in line with the development of the *internet and the many instruments of communication destined to become indispensable in everyone's daily lives* (Eurydice 2000: xxi).

As for the perceived educational benefits associated with ICT, it has been suggested they include:

♦ Enhanced physical development (for example, hand: eye co-ordination and fine motor control);

The Drive to Include ICT in Early Years Practice

- Improving and increasing children's knowledge and understanding of the world around them (encouraging *flexibility and openness of mind*);
- Particular benefits from *assistive technologies* for children with special educational needs (Pierce 1994).

The National Association of Advisers for Computers in Education (NAACE) and the British Educational Communications and Technology Agency (BECTa) produced a joint discussion document in 2001 aimed at stimulating debate on the key characteristics of good quality teaching and learning with ICT. This document proposed five features of effective practice associated with enhancing ICT capability and the development of metacognitive abilities (learning to learn). The exemplar material given in support of these features covered classes of children throughout the primary and secondary age phases, although not the early years (Figure 1).

In England and Wales the government acted on its belief in the importance of ICT, pressing ahead with the introduction and development of the National Grid for Learning (NGfL) and allocating large sums of money to support the increased use of computers in teaching and learning (Revell 2001a). Although the spending emphasis to date has leant heavily towards equipment purchases (Eurydice 2000), these increases in resourcing have also been accompanied by developments in curriculum design. ICT in the National Curriculum has evolved from a cross-curricular skill and adjunct to the Design and Technology Programme of Study (DES 1989) to a *de facto* subject in its own right (QCA 1999).

Feature	Characteristics
Autonomy	The use of ICT can promote the development of pupil autonomy and independence as learners. It offers opportunities for children to take some control over their learning, either independently or collaboratively, working at a pace and level appropriate to the child (NAACE/BECTa 2001: 2).
	Example – 6 and 7 year olds preparing a presentation on *Our Home Town* remember using a digital camera in previous work and ask the teacher for it again in order to record some of their ideas for the presentation.
Capability	The incorporation of ICT into the curriculum enables children to acquire the knowledge and skills necessary to make effective use of new technologies (learning about ICT) and to be able to transfer these capabilities to support learning in other areas of the curriculum (learning through ICT) (NAACE/BECTa 2001: 5).
	Example – 6 and 7 year olds reordering a mixed up fairy story into the correct sequence using the word processor; selecting sentences, cutting and pasting, altering font sizes and styles.
Creativity	ICT has the potential to inspire creativity in children by providing access to empowering tools (NAACE/BECTa 2001: 8).
	Examples – 6 and 7 year olds using a drawing package to do an observational drawing; selecting colours and brush types, filling in shapes and editing pictures in a way that would be almost impossible with other media.

Feature	Characteristics
Quality	ICT has the potential to enhance the quality of finished products both in terms of their appearance and presentation, but also in terms of enriching children's ideas through access to an enhanced range of source material (NAACE/BECTa 2001: 9).
	Example – 5 and 6 year olds sorting and matching shapes and colours using the My World package, with some adding their own titles and text before printing out the results for a wall display for parents.
Scope	ICT offers children access to learning activities and experiences that would not be possible in any other way (NAACE/BECTa 2001: 11).
	Example – 5 6 year olds making use of the replay facility on a CD-ROM in order to listen and read more than once thereby reinforcing meaning. In this way children can check their understanding and work at their own pace.

Figure 1

Developments in the early years

As with the National Curriculum for primary and secondary pupils, the development of national documentation for early years (age 3–5) settings in England and Wales has increasingly recognised a role for ICT in teaching and learning (SCAA 1996; QCA 2000). The review of the Desirable Outcomes for children's learning on entering compulsory education (QCA 1998; SMSR Ltd. 1999) made little mention of ICT beyond stating that some respondents felt that it should be given greater emphasis (QCA 1998: 5). An

all-encompassing statement such as *use technology, where appropriate, to support their learning* (SCAA 1996) offered little or no insight into desirable ICT practice in nurseries and reception classes, and did nothing to correct the possible erroneous conflation of ICT with computers in many people's minds. The subsequent introduction in England and Wales of the Curriculum guidance for the foundation stage (QCA 2000) did not include a separate area of learning devoted to ICT, but it did offer increased detail on suitable ICT experiences for young children.

Areas of learning such as Mathematical development (QCA 2000: 80) or Communication, language and literacy (QCA 2000: 63) are identified as containing opportunities for the employment of ICT as a resource to support teaching and learning. These opportunities include listening to taped stories in a small group, instructing a programmable vehicle such as the Pixie, or working with CD-ROM talking books on the computer. Statements relating to appropriate learning in ICT are also present under the heading of: Knowledge and understanding of the world (QCA 2000: 92–3). The statements include *showing an interest in ICT, learning how to operate simple equipment*, and eventually, *performing simple functions on ICT and computer equipment*. These stepping stones and their accompanying examples are intended to guide practitioners in assisting children to attain the early learning goal (ELG) of being able to *recognize everyday uses of ICT and use ICT to support their learning* (QCA 2000: 92).

Alongside the undoubted increase in the

incidence of new technologies in nurseries and schools (Revell 2001a) and the developments in curriculum design (QCA 2000), there has also been a debate as to the rationale for including ICT in early years provision. Some (Elkind 1996; NAEYC 1996; Anderson 2000; Siraj-Blatchford and Siraj-Blatchford 2002) have sought to ensure primacy for developmentally (rather than socially, culturally or economically) appropriate uses for the technology in early years settings. A useful and accessible summary of what developmental appropriateness means and what the implications might be for early years practice can be located on the Developmentally Appropriate Technology for Early Childhood website (www.ioe.ac.uk/cdl/datec). In the United States the National Association for the Education of Young Children (NAEYC) has also categorised ICT as a new tool that could and should be incorporated into existing early years practice, but only in developmentally appropriate ways; supplementing, but not replacing, important first-hand experiences and interactions (NAEYC 1996). NAEYC reminded early years practitioners everywhere that there could be a considerable disparity between a child's ICT skills and their comprehension of what is happening. For example, the young child whose mouse handling skills are competent, but who resorts to touching the computer screen directly in an attempt to rectify a mistaken command.

If early years education is a distinctive phase in its own right (DfEE 1997a; QCA 2000) and not merely a preparatory stage for primary and

secondary schooling, then practitioners may well argue that the priority is to provide young children with an educational experience that corresponds to their needs today, rather than to a set of anticipated needs at some undetermined point in the future. That said, developmental appropriateness and social, cultural or economic relevance are not necessarily mutually exclusive. Perhaps the best way to prepare children for tomorrow *is* to give them what they need today (Nutbrown 1996).

Other writers on the subject of ICT in early years education have, however, been much more hostile to the introduction of some new technologies into early years settings, believing that the benefits have been grossly overstated while at the same time the costs have been underplayed (McVeigh and Paton Walsh 2000). Some forms of ICT have been described as inherently unsuitable for application in early years education (Alliance for Childhood 2000). Computers in particular have been viewed as inappropriate tools that risk *stunting children's intelligence and social skills – and may be damaging their health* (McVeigh and Paton Walsh 2000). For such commentators and practitioners the intro-duction of computers is felt to fly in the face of good early years practice and what are currently accepted as the needs of young children, including first-hand experience, play and talk. Critics have cited the potentially inimical effects of prolonged computer use on young children in terms of their physical and social well being (Oppenheimer 1997; Meltz 1998; Kelly 2000; McVeigh and Paton Walsh 2000). Over preoccupation with computers may

impede the establishment of good social skills and concern for others, the inculcation of which early years practitioners rightly regard as an important part of their role (Alliance for Childhood 2000). Concerns have also been raised about potential hidden health costs as a result of young children spending too much time on the computer and using equipment designed for adult bodies such as:

- Vision strain;
- Radiation / cancer risks;
- Repetitive strain injuries;
- Sedentary lifestyles leading to obesity.

Commentary

If the purpose of educational reform is to improve pupil achievement and attainment then ultimately this depends upon what teachers and children do in nurseries and classrooms (Crossley 2000). While the power to adopt a particular education policy rests ultimately with the policy-makers, the power to implement it rests in large part with the practitioners. From an early years perspective, the five features articulated in the NAACE/BECTa document (2001) appear to contain other features that are implicit or embedded within them. Given the philosophy underpinning much early years practice, particularly the rationale for playing and talking as central features of good practice, working with ICT could be seen to offer young children an additional context in which to develop their interpersonal, communication and thinking skills. If used appropriately, ICT might make a contribution to children's personal, social and emotional development as a result of their involvement in collaborative activities with new technologies. ICT may also offer opportunities for children to think about and debate what could or should be done and how to do it; for example, working out how to get a programmable vehicle to go from A to B. Children may have to allocate roles, tasks and equipment when using ICT, they may need to monitor what is going on and respond when things do not go according to plan. The potential for developing children's communication, language and literacy skills as a result of collaborative play activities appears considerable.

A frequent claim made in support of the educational value of ICT cites the power it has to motivate, excite and enthuse children. Certainly the appearance of something new in an early years setting can create considerable interest and excitement amongst young children, although this is hardly peculiar to ICT, and it remains to be seen whether the excitement created by ICT has a unique or particular longevity. That said, work with ICT can provide a new context for practitioners to encourage children to ask questions, offer opinions and justifications, consider a range of options, seek the ideas and opinions of their friends and come to conclusions and agreements. If young children learn in part through their discussions and interactions with peers and adults then the potential of ICT to promote talk and collaboration could constitute significant reasons for its inclusion in an early years curriculum (Cooper and Brna 2002).

ICT is not a substitute for tried and tested activities and first-hand experiences but offers a means of extending and enhancing those experiences and activities. For example, providing children with experience of observational artwork using traditional media and then introducing paint packages using the computer. Many early years practitioners have already made practical use of ICT in teaching and learning (Reidy 1992; Appleyard 1997; Grenier 1999; Benjamin 2000) and are engaged in innovative practice using ICT based on their understanding of the needs and characteristics of young children (Matthews and Jessel 1993; Baker 1999; Vandervelde 1999; Freedman 2001). The sources cited above show practitioners exercising their professional judgement about what ICT is appropriate for the children, developing learning environments in such a way as to encourage its use, and getting involved in that use in order to help children learn *about* as well as *through* the technology.

Generally, however, in the context of nursery and reception classes ICT has had a less than well-developed identity and many teachers have expressed concerns over their own level of skills and the knowledge needed to make effective use of the technologies (The Stevenson Report 1997; Ofsted 2000). There is a good deal of evidence from recent years that raises serious question marks over the implementation of ICT policy in respect of early years education in England and Wales (Ofsted

2000; Moyles *et al.* 2002). The Office for Standards in Education (Ofsted) reported in 1995 that teacher competence with ICT and their ability to make the best use of the technology in their teaching needed considerable strengthening. Two years after this assessment The Stevenson Report (1997) cautioned against premature increases in hardware in schools due to the existing state of skills and confidence among many practitioners coupled with the shortage of appropriate software. Although no specific reference to nurseries was included in its assessment of the contemporary context and the measures required to remedy the situation, The Stevenson Report did make clear the wide range of experience, knowledge, skills and attitudes among teachers in general in relation to ICT.

Concerns about the effective delivery of the ICT curriculum in the primary sector and the parlous state of some teachers' subject knowledge were still in evidence in 1998-99 (Ofsted 2000) despite the improvement in equipment levels and the operation of some extra-curricular provision. All that could be said of the experiences of under-fives in the maintained sector was that most children had experienced using a computer (Ofsted 2000) and that many nurseries had difficulties in providing adequate computer resources. More recently, Ofsted reported that one in five primary schools, in which reception classes are located, were found not to be delivering National Curriculum requirements in terms of ICT (Revell 2001b). Since then the Study of Pedagogical Effectiveness in Early Learning (SPEEL) (Moyles *et al.* 2002) and the

The Drive to Include ICT in Early Years Practice

Researching Effective Pedagogy in the Early Years (EPPE) (Siraj-Blatchford *et al.* 2002) projects have both identified ICT as an area for further development in early years education.

A practitioner who remains unconvinced about the appropriateness of ICT in early years education or who is unhappy about her/his own ICT capability could produce a significant mismatch between the official policy and the actual experiences of young children. Much of the reform concerning ICT and early years education in England and Wales, for example, has tended to concentrate (thus far at least) on curriculum design and resourcing (Davitt 2000) and these structural changes may not have much impact upon day-to-day teaching practice. In some settings an observer may well see practice that is patchy and uneven (Haughton 2000) with, for example, the computer used more as a free-standing activity or time-filler rather than a valued resource for the promotion of children's learning and development (Smidt 2002). Where adult intervention does take place, it may not extend much beyond basic instruction on how to use a software package, switching on a computer, loading programs, or fixing it when it crashes. There may even be an assumption that the technology can be relied upon to do the teaching as with some drill and skill software. Attempts to explain patchy and uneven practice sometimes draw on a deficit model of practitioners. Such models highlight a series of inhibiting factors at work (Figure 2), factors which might be overcome through the provision of ICT skills training coupled with qualitative and

ICT in the Early Years

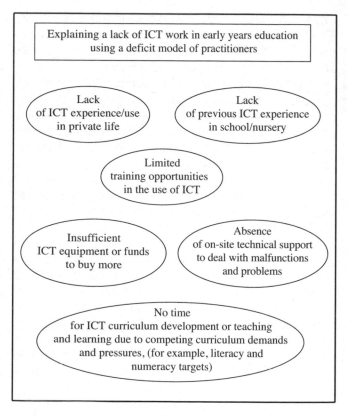

Explaining a lack of ICT work in early years education using a deficit model of practitioners

Lack of ICT experience/use in private life

Lack of previous ICT experience in school/nursery

Limited training opportunities in the use of ICT

Insufficient ICT equipment or funds to buy more

Absence of on-site technical support to deal with malfunctions and problems

No time for ICT curriculum development or teaching and learning due to competing curriculum demands and pressures, (for example, literacy and numeracy targets)

Figure 2

quantitative improvements in equipment (Ofsted 2000; Kenny 2001; Revell 2001b).

The deficits outlined in Figure 2 may well exist in varying measure. Ofsted has been critical of the availability of technical support and the ineffectual nature of some of the New Opportunities Fund

(NOF) ICT training for existing staff (Kenny 2001). Concern has also been raised about the impact of competing policy pressures on schools in England and Wales, particularly the pressures of literacy and numeracy hours (Revell 2001b). However there is a danger of assuming that any apparent teacher *resistance* to an increased prominence for ICT in the early years is primarily skills and resources dependent as this could mask more fundamental pedagogical concerns amongst practitioners. Dawes (1999) points out that the reasons why ICT may not feature as expected in schools may have less to do with stereotypical views of practitioners as technically fearful, inept and incapable, but result instead from professional judgements about the appropriateness of ICT in educational settings. Narrow definitions of ICT that focus primarily upon computers and drill and skill software could contribute to this kind of professional judgement. In Dawes' view some teachers at least are making choices and decisions concerning the use of new technologies based on their beliefs about good practice, rather than fears about their own capabilities.

Clearly it takes time for new resources and systems to take effect. It may take even longer to raise the confidence and capability of some practitioners and in other cases overcome pedagogical doubts about the relevance of the technology (Revell 2001a; Kenny 2001; Haughton 2000). The fact remains that some practitioners at least remain to be convinced of the potential and scope of ICT in early years education (Siraj-

Blatchford *et al.* 2002; Moyles *et al.* 2002). While research into the value and worth of ICT in early years learning environments is starting to be conducted (Siraj-Blatchford and Siraj-Blatchford 2001) the relative recency of the technology means that there is much to be learnt. In the meantime early years practitioners find themselves required to introduce ICT to their children *now* and so practical ways forward are needed and the following sections offer some examples of ICT work in nursery and reception classes followed by discussion and commentary. The discussion draws on existing knowledge about young children as learners, the organization and management of early years learning environments, and the role of the practitioner in early years education in an attempt to make suggestions about teaching and learning involving ICT in early years settings. The examples used involve work in both reception (4–5-years-old) and nursery (3–4-years-old) settings.

The reception examples took place during a Summer term. A number of themes, some related, others discrete, were planned, the majority of which were seasonally driven (Figure 3). The weather, Summer time, travel and holidays all featured strongly. Arising out of the travel and holiday strand was early science and technology work on moving and forces. The work also coincided with the football World Cup taking place in South Korea and Japan which the children were very interested in. The whole school was including work on Japan at various points during the second half of the term. In these examples ICT was

The Drive to Include ICT in Early Years Practice

Reception		Half term	HT	HT	HT	HT	HT	HT
Knowledge and understanding of the world			**1**	**2**	**3**	**4**	**5**	**6**

Week	Science	Geography/ History	Design Technology/ ICT		
1	Signs of summer	The weather			
2	Seaside things Pushes and pulls	Journeys	Transport (cars) – ramps and controlled vehicles/Roamer Seaside café (electronic till, CCTV, calculators, telephone)		
3	Floating and sinking		Transport (boats) – sand and water play		
4		Holidays (around the world)	Transport (planes) – small world activities Photographs using digital camera		
5	Shadows and shadow puppets	Japanese week	Designing and making lamps, clothing, food Karaoke concert		
6		Travel agents	Aeroplane role-play area, seatbelt signs, in-flight entertainment system (listening station), walkie-talkies		

Figure 3

integrated into the planning and provision for Knowledge and understanding of the world (QCA 2000: 82–99) although there were also links with other aspects of the early years curriculum including creative development and personal and social development.

The nursery examples took place during Autumn and Spring terms. The main theme for the Autumn term was Festivals and Celebrations, which was designed to draw on the children's experiences of events such as Hannukah, Divali and Christmas as festivals of light. The nursery team had also developed a discrete programme for ICT that ran alongside but was not wholly linked to the main theme (Figure 4).

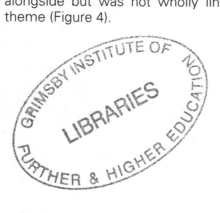

GRIMSBY INSTITUTE OF LIBRARIES FURTHER & HIGHER EDUCATION

The Drive to Include ICT in Early Years Practice

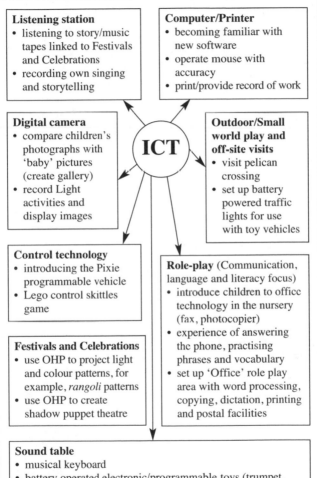

Listening station
- listening to story/music tapes linked to Festivals and Celebrations
- recording own singing and storytelling

Computer/Printer
- becoming familiar with new software
- operate mouse with accuracy
- print/provide record of work

Digital camera
- compare children's photographs with 'baby' pictures (create gallery)
- record Light activities and display images

ICT

Outdoor/Small world play and off-site visits
- visit pelican crossing
- set up battery powered traffic lights for use with toy vehicles

Control technology
- introducing the Pixie programmable vehicle
- Lego control skittles game

Role-play (Communication, language and literacy focus)
- introduce children to office technology in the nursery (fax, photocopier)
- experience of answering the phone, practising phrases and vocabulary
- set up 'Office' role play area with word processing, copying, dictation, printing and postal facilities

Festivals and Celebrations
- use OHP to project light and colour patterns, for example, *rangoli* patterns
- use OHP to create shadow puppet theatre

Sound table
- musical keyboard
- battery operated electronic/programmable toys (trumpet, saxophone, guitar, music mat)

Figure 4: Nursery–Autumn Term

2

ICT and Young Children as Learners

Examples

Age: Reception
Location: Carpeted area and outdoor area
Activity: Introducing the walkie-talkies

Six children are sitting in the quiet area with an adult who
introduces a pair of walkie-talkies.
Adult: (Holding up a walkie-talkie.) 'Does anyone know what this
is?'
D: 'I've got those at home.'
A: 'It's a phone!'
Adult: 'It does look like a mobile phone doesn't it. It's a bit like a
phone too. It's called a walkie-talkie and you can use it to radio
people. You press the button and say something, then you let the
button go to listen and the other person can radio you back. Would
anyone like to have a go?'
Chorus of 'Yes', 'Me please', one child (C) shakes her head to
indicate 'No'.
Adult produces three pairs of walkie-talkies from the tray and
passes them to the children who want to try. C is invited/
encouraged to sit with the adult to watch the others for a while.
The children experiment with the walkie-talkies becoming
increasingly excited.
A: (Presses send button.) 'Hello B it's A, can you hear me?'
(Keeps pressing the send button.)
B: 'YES! Can you hear me?'
Adult: 'A, if you let go of the button when you've spoken you'll be
able to hear the reply.'
D: (Clutching groin and dancing around with excitement.) 'May

Day! May Day! Ha Ha.'

A,B,C,E & F: 'Ha Ha Ha. Look at D.'

Adult: (Smiling) 'That's very good D, what does May Day mean?'

D: 'It means they're going to crash.' (Speaking into radio again.) 'May Day! May Day! May Day! Ha Ha.'

Adult to C: 'Would you like to have a go now?'

C: (Nods and smiles but says nothing.)

Adult passes C the spare walkie-talkie and asks B to work with her.

Adult to C and B: 'Can you hear each other? Yes? Excellent.'

After two or three minutes C holds out the radio to the adult indicating she has had enough.

Adult: 'Have you finished C?' (C nods.) 'OK well done, shall I put the walkie-talkie back in the box for now? Are you going to come and sit with me again?'

E: (Presses send button, then talks very loudly into the ear piece.) 'CAN ANYONE HEAR ME?'

Adult: 'I think we can all hear you E! When you speak, try talking into this bit and put your ear next to this bit. Then you'll be able to hear them. Try it again.'

E tries again.

Adult to F: 'Can you hear E? Try saying something back.'

F: 'Hello E I can hear you, can you hear me?'

B to Adult: 'This one's making a funny noise.'

Adult: 'Is it? Can I have a listen? Oh yes, it sounds all scratchy. I think it might be feedback. I think you might be too close to each other.'

A to E: 'You go into a different room!'

E: 'No let's go out here (points to outdoor area) it'll be better.'

Adult: 'That's a good idea. Let's go and try outside where there's a bit more room and we won't disturb other people.'

Figure 5

Age: Reception
Location: Socio-dramatic role play area
Activity: Multiple uses of ICT in The Travel Agents/Aeroplane

As part of the Summer time themes being explored in the classroom the socio-dramatic role play area was extended to incorporate a travel agent and an aeroplane. The travel agents included a non-functioning PC for the children to check prices and availability, an electronic cash register, calculators and a telephone as well as catalogues and a globe. The aeroplane was constructed from sheets of cardboard donated by a parent, painted and laced together using string. The class PC was placed in the cockpit and some simple controls made from found materials were placed in front of the screen. While the children were flying the aeroplane the PC was used to show photographs of clouds located on the internet to give the impression of looking out of the windscreen. The multiple tape player/listening station was placed in the passenger cabin with a number of sets of headphones and acted as an in-flight entertainment system. There was also a simple homemade battery powered seatbelt sign manufactured by a classroom helper and operated by a simple on/off switch. This allowed the 'cabin staff' to tell passengers when to strap themselves in for take-off and landing. The class teacher had discussed holiday destinations with the children prior to setting up the area and many of the children had first-hand experience of flying. Children booked their flights in the travel agents and then went through the door into the cabin and took their seats.

Adult: 'Oh hello. I wondered if I could book a holiday.'
A: 'Yes, where do you want to go? You can go to Tenerife if you want. I went there with my mum and dad.'
Adult: 'Oh did you. Well that sounds good. How much is it?'
A jabs numbers into a calculator.
A: 'It's £426.'
Adult: 'Well that sounds very reasonable. I've got the money here.' (Hands over paper 'money' which A places in the till.)
A then begins to type rapidly on the computer keyboard.
Adult: 'What are you writing?'

A: 'I'm not *writing*! I'm *typing* and I'm going to send a fax to the plane to stop it because someone's missed the flight.'
Adult: 'Oh, good idea.'
A: 'I've been to Cyprus too.'
Adult: 'Have you?
A: 'Yes. I know where Cyprus is.' (Picks up globe.) 'It's here.' (By luck or by judgement, points at the Mediterranean.)
Adult: 'Yes that's right!'
A: 'Do you know this shows you the whole world? That's the North Pole and that's the South Pole, and you can find your way round with a compass. Do you know where Hawaii is?'
Adult: 'Urm, I think it's round the other side of the world.' (Rotates globe.) 'There it is, look.' (Pointing.)
A: 'Oh yes. Where's Hornsea then? My Gran lives in Hornsea. Is Hornsea a little country?'

Once in the passenger cabin clutching a ticket the adult notices three girls serving in-flight meals to a group of boys all of whom are listening to taped music on the in-flight entertainment system. Meanwhile in the cockpit the pilot and co-pilot (both girls) have managed to quell the disruptive behaviour of two more of the boys who were threatening to derail their play by telling them that they should be dogs and that they should go to sleep in the corner. Whereupon the 'dogs' duly curl up and the flight resumes.

Figure 6

Cognitive development

The work of developmental psychologists such as Piaget (Bruce 1997), Isaacs (Isaacs 1929, 1932, 1951), Bruner (Wood 1998), Donaldson (Donaldson 1978), Vygotsky (Bruce 1997; Wood 1998) and others has made a significant impact on early years practitioners' understanding of children as learners during the last century. For Piaget, children were not miniature adults in terms of their cognitive abilities. He postulated a series of developmental stages that children went through in regular and ordered sequence; sensorimotor, pre-operational, concrete operational and formal operational (Donaldson 1978). A key element of Piaget's ideas that distinguished him from earlier behaviourist psychologists was the belief that children actively construct meaning, rather than being the *tabula rasa* envisaged in some previous models of childhood. For Piaget, young children assimilate knowledge as a result of first-hand experience and play. Subsequent experience forces a child to re-evaluate her/his original ideas in the light of new situations and observations in order to accommodate to the new reality (Bruce 1997). The intellectual disequilibrium that results from new and different situations is resolved as new information and is incorporated into, or used to supplant, old ideas. In each of the stages set out in the Piagetian model children are believed to refine their thinking in the light of experience as part of a sequence that is invariable; children cannot bypass stages or make short cuts to reach more advanced levels of thinking.

One result of this interactionist view of learning and development has been the development of early years curricula in which children are perceived as active learners who benefit from first-hand experience in meaningful situations. This belief in the value of first-hand experience has led some commentators to express concern about some forms of ICT, notably computers, as a result of the apparent replacement of first-hand experience with virtual experience (McVeigh and Paton Walsh 2000; Alliance for Childhood 2000). Yet computers do not have to mean unsupported, low level drill and skill exercises (Siraj-Blatchford and Siraj-Blatchford 2001). Figure 6 shows computers integrated into socio-dramatic role-play and as Cooper and Brna have argued (2002), sensitive intervention on the part of knowledgeable adults can help children to learn *about* ICT and *through* ICT in ways that are appropriate and meaningful.

Like Piaget, Bruner also developed a stage model to explain children's cognitive development. However, Bruner suggested that children were capable of intellectual achievements at an earlier point than that predicted by Piaget as a result of instruction and carefully structured learning environments. For Bruner, children's progress through play and first-hand experience can be *scaffolded* by adults who are effective at questioning, guiding and instructing in ways that will extend and challenge children's thinking (Wood 1998). Similarly, Vygotsky's concept of a zone of proximal development (ZPD) which represented the gap between what children can do with and without assistance from more knowledgeable individuals (Bruce 1997) was another attempt to signal the importance of language and social interaction in cognitive development. For social-interactionists such as Bruner and Vygotsky, working collaboratively and co-operatively constitute an important learning mechanism (Bruce 1997). In the context of ICT for example, this could include one child teaching another child how a piece of technology works, resulting in learning for both children. The role-play area in Figure 6 proved to be fertile ground for discussion and social interaction while Figures 9 and 16 (p. 42 and p. 66) show adult intervention being used to guide and challenge children's thinking as well as extending their ICT capabilities.

The whole child

Any explanatory model of childhood needs to make reference to the whole child. Many researchers have pointed out that children are *made up of far more than cognitive capacities* (Zigler in Hyson 1994: ix). Just as there is a relationship between thought and action, so too is there a reciprocal relationship between thought and feeling. Susan Isaacs' work at the Malting House School from 1924 onwards was important in carrying forward the theoretical basis of early years education. Isaacs' scientifically based inclusion of an affective dimension to the nature of childhood helped to ensure that young children were seen as more than just cognitive beings. Isaacs' work provided a rational theoretical underpinning for the importance of personal and social development and the need for children to exercise responsibility and choice in order to develop independence, autonomy and self-control.

This important idea that children are not simply cognitive beings but are also emotional and social ones, and that furthermore there is a connection between growth and development in the first area, and growth and development in the second area (Isaacs 1951) is significant. A child's social development will effect the way they relate to peers and adults. Whilst patterns of behaviour with others (peers and adults) will already be in evidence when children start nursery/reception, early years practitioners have a big part to play in influencing the continuing social development of a child. Collaborative work involving ICT in all its forms may offer new opportunities for doing this (Cooper and Brna 2002). Introducing children to ICT in interesting and imaginative ways could therefore provide children with new and different experiences of:

- Experimenting, trying things out and being prepared to make mistakes;
- Persevering when things do not work first time round;
- Coping with things going awry;
- Acquiring new skills;
- Joining in and enjoying working with others.

Bruce's ten principles of early years care and education (1997) acknowledge the emotional/cognitive link and the positive emotional bases of children's self-initiated learning. These include satisfied curiosity; pleasure in finding out; the intrinsic reward of mastery; identification with adults and teachers; and the impact of adult praise, recognition, confidence and trust (Hyson 1994). Memory and learning may well be enhanced in settings that heighten interest and happiness, enabling greater tolerance of frustration and promoting perseverance.

Some researchers have argued that for children to be successful learners they need to develop a series of *super skills*. For some these have been characterised as motivation; socialization; confidence (Ball in Keenan 2002), for others as learning dispositions; respect for self and others; and emotional well being (Pascal *et al.* in Keenan 2002). Learning dispositions include such skills and attitudes as resilience, organizational skills, curiosity, concentration, inventiveness, self-management and openness. The characteristics of play, exploratory and/or social in nature, make this an ideal way to develop super skills. Play could be seen as a natural process through which children learn about the physical world around them (Bruce 1997). Through play children can experience making choices; take responsibility for their learning; act out feelings; encounter and take on board new ideas; have opportunities to learn through movement and the use of all the senses; engage in long-term, in-depth exploration; and draw all the above together to make sense of the world (Bruce 1997).

As play constitutes a central pillar of learning in the early years it seems probable that a play-based approach to ICT will be an important feature of efforts to improve young children's skills and confidence in this area (Siraj-Blatchford and Siraj-Blatchford 2001). While people expecting formal teaching methods may see play-based approaches as *random informality* they are instead *carefully structured situations* in which children work with peers, adults, or alone, to master important skills, concepts and attitudes (Keenan 2002). Young children may enjoy using a programmable toy, a paint programme, playing with a computer keyboard and watching what happens on screen when different keys are pressed, or as with the children in Figure 5, talking to one another using the walkie-talkies. Although to the untrained eye this type of activity may appear little more than *messing about*, this physical exploration is an important part of learning for young children (Smidt 2002).

In Figure 5 the children were certainly very excited by the novel resources. This excitement lasted throughout the session and the quality of the play was relatively low at first as they wrestled with the mechanics of getting the equipment to work properly. Indeed the conversations did not get much beyond 'Hello' and 'Can you hear me?'. A similar observation was made in relation to Figure 14 (see p. 63). Four weeks later however, two of the children from the original group were observed in the aeroplane role-play area featured in Figure 6. They were using the walkie-talkies again, this time however the novelty had worn off and they were integrating the equipment into an imaginative play situation much more effectively by talking to one another about a plane coming in to land. The introduction of new technologies may result in high levels of excitement initially, accompanied by a temporary reduction in play quality. However, once some of the children had had time to develop the skills and familiarity with the technology the quality of their play returned, with the added dimension of ICT attached.

Diversity: young children as individuals

Questions remain over the universal applicability of theories on the nature of childhood developed in western societies. Seeing young children as individuals is important in that it foreshadows the idea that children vary as a result of age, maturity, culture, class, gender, ethnicity, education and/or parenting (David 1998; Early Childhood Education Forum, 1998). Western developmental notions of childhood that apply the concept of incompetence, or *becoming*, in undifferentiated ways to children at various ages run the risk of ignoring the influence of social, economic and cultural factors (Mason and Steadman 1996). Susan Isaacs identified a series of factors in the 1920s and 1930s that could play a role in determining individual differences, including inborn ability, temperament and character, as well as home and social background (Isaacs 1951). The environment in which a child grows, including cultural, social and economic factors, influences her/his social and emotional development (Keinbaum and Trommsdorff 1999). As the relationship between cognitive and social and emotional development is iterative this could have consequences for teaching and learning with and about ICT in the early years.

The childhoods experienced by children in different locations or from different family backgrounds are unlikely to be identical. They will have had all manner of experiences before they enter an educational setting of any kind and are likely to display a range of pre-dispositions. Some will have special educational needs (SEN) including physical disabilities, learning difficulties or behavioural problems, others may be gifted or talented in some way. Some children will have experienced home environments rich in language, having had stories read to them; exposure to a wide vocabulary; and being allowed or encouraged to ask questions. Others will not. Some children will have the self-confidence and esteem that comes from receiving praise and recognition from parents. They may have experience of mixing with different adults and peers, or have been encouraged to get involved in activities which offer practice in co-operation, listening, concentrating, waiting, sharing and turn taking. Others will not. Similar disparities in previous experience with ICT are equally likely.

When it comes to ICT not all children will be starting from the same point. Some children will have had much more extensive experience of ICT, having used televisions, VCRs, telephones, PCs, or programmable toys. Others will not. In Figure 5 some of the children quickly grasped the technique, which end of the walkie-talkie to speak into, which end to listen to, when to press the *send* button and when to let go and listen. At least one child had previous experience of using the technology in play situations in the home. At the same time other children found it much harder to get the devices to work properly and spoke into the wrong end or kept their fingers on the *send* button making it impossible to receive any messages. One of the children was quite nervous and rendered uncertain by the new resources. It was important to be sensitive to these feelings and not to push or pressurize the child into participation before she felt confident enough to do so. Once she had watched the other children playing and enjoying themselves for a while she felt sufficiently emboldened to have a go, albeit only for a few minutes. This was an achievement on her part and was recognized as such.

If universal theories of childhood are not the whole story then we may expect to find that not all children are equally eager to investigate and learn in situations involving the use of ICT. While many children may be happy to explore and gain ICT experience, others may fear that experience, suspecting the worst in new situations as in Figure 5 (Hyson 1994). The experiences of children whose parents have provided them with access to ICT at home may not offer much insight into the experiences and development of children without such opportunities. Similarly, the types of ICT available at home may also influence the types of attitudes and skills that emerge in schools and nurseries. Economic, social and cultural factors may mean that the technological dimension of childhood is significantly different for, for example, rich and poor, male and female (Passig and Levin 2000). MacNaughton's work (1997) in Australia on boys' and girls' choices of play areas and their use of space and time has shown how there is a tendency on the part of some boys to challenge or deny access to some types of play, such as construction play, on male terms. Although MacNaughton's focus was not ICT, there could be parallels (see

Figure 7 below). Young children can pick up and adopt notions of male and female roles and activities at an early age and ICT, particularly computers, may well carry connotations of *toys for the boys*. Given the possible gendered image that ICT may have, this could well be an important area for consideration by practitioners when planning for ICT in early years settings.

John and Helen (Y1) were asked to produce a piece of writing on the computer. The teacher noticed that John had occupied the seat in front of the keyboard and was monopolising the activity. The teacher intervened and informed John that it was a joint task and that Helen needed to have a go on the computer too. The teacher then moved on to work with another group of children. John meanwhile sat back in his seat with his arms folded. Helen had to reach across him to get to the keyboard. Before long Helen's exclusion was reimposed. (O'Hara 2000:136)

Figure 7

Figure 6 does seem to suggest that in some circumstances at least some boys and some girls will behave in stereotypical ways when encountering ICT. Three of the girls became air stewardesses, waiting on a small group of male passengers who had commandeered the in-flight entertainment system. At the same time some of the boys began acting disruptively and boisterously in the cockpit where two girls were engaged in imaginative play involving the controls and the PC. Practitioners will need to consider whether similar patterns exist when activities involving ICT are taking place in their own settings (Early Childhood

Education Forum 1998). This said, the fact that childhoods can be so very different mean it is dangerous to make sweeping assertions about boys' and girls' behaviour. When it comes to ICT not all young girls will be *powerless* and not all young boys will be *powerful*. Such a high degree of homogeneity among boys and girls seems unlikely. The female pilot and co-pilot in Figure 6 appeared to have a highly effective means of managing the boys' behaviour and retaining their control of the equipment. Once they had adopted the proffered role of *dogs* the boys were then compelled by the rules of the game to act like dogs (Keenan 2002), in other words, *'In your basket and lie down!'*.

If a judgement is reached that there is indeed an issue relating to access and inclusion the question remains as to what to do about it. MacNaughton (1997) evaluated teacher strategies for dealing with stereotypical behaviour in relation to construction play and found problems with many of them, both in terms of their underlying assumptions about the nature of the problem and their efficacy as a palliative. MacNaughton suggests that *feminization* (luring girls into non-traditional areas with *girls* things) and *separatism* (girls only time), are premised on the belief that the problem lies with the girls and sparking their interest. At the same time *fusion* (combining *boys* with *girls* areas) and *policing* (adult intervention) are responses to a problem that lies with boys' unacceptable behaviour and requires adult mediation in the interests of equity. In each case the strategies require com-mitment and ongoing monitoring and involvement on the part of practitioners. When the monitoring and involvement was reduced, previously established patterns of behaviour tended to re-establish themselves. For MacNaughton young children are trying hard to be *normal* therefore practitioners need to broaden children's ideas of what is normal for boys and girls (1997).

In spite of the qualifications that have been added to the developmental theories above, Blenkin and Kelly (2000) have argued convincingly that by taking a more holistic view of childhood it is possible to discern a period of *infancy* in which children do have some needs in common. Children's development does appear to be broadly sequential in nature with things happening in a particular order, an order that to all intents and purposes is the same for all children (Sharman *et al.* 1995). As such, it is possible to set out principles of good practice provided that practitioners remember that children are individuals and are likely to be at different points in their development and learning. Practitioners have to bear in mind that:

◆ The rate of children's development can vary widely;

◆ These differing rates of development are the product of a range of factors that include environmental, social, cultural, personal, biological and economic elements;

◆ Some of these factors can enhance and promote a child's development, while others will hinder and inhibit it (QCA 2000: 6).

ICT and Young Children as Learners

The plans, practices and expectations of early years practitioners have to be informed by an understanding of where the children are at in terms of their ICT knowledge and skills and their prior exposure to, and experience of, ICT. Practitioners need to gauge where the children's strengths lie in terms of super skills and learning dispositions (Keenan 2002) and in what areas they experience difficulties (QCA 2000).

3

Planning for ICT and Organizing the Learning Environment

Examples

Age: Nursery
Location: Socio-dramatic role-play area
Activity: Using the PC in imaginative play in The Office

A: (Picks up the telephone receiver and begins a quiet conversation with an imaginary caller.)

B: (Lifts the photocopier lid, places a drawing face down and closes lid. Presses a series of buttons. Lifts lid again, takes out the drawing and offers it to an adult.) 'It's copied.'

C: (Approaches the computer keyboard having watched other children first. Keys in the letter L and looks up at the screen. She smiles and points at the letter.) 'It's the same!'

D: (Types furiously on the computer keyboard for a short time, then grabs the nearest adult.) 'I want numbers now!'
Adult: 'There's some numbers there on the keyboard. Try pressing those.'
D: (Presses a few numbers and then returns to random letters and symbols. Points at the screen.) 'That's my name!'
Adult: 'Oh, have you written your name? Can you read it to me?'
D: (Points to the screen showing:
DFGHJKLL;POYREW2W21ZRYUJK,MNBVC14789-632ACDKG
'Helen!' (Pause) 'Where's my photo?'
Adult: 'Your photo?'
D: 'Yes.' (Pointing to the printer.) 'It won't come out!'

Adult: 'Oh, you want to *print* it out. Here, let me help you.'
D: (Peers into the printer's innards to observe the mechanism at work.) 'It's coming!' (Printed sheet drops into the tray.) 'Hooray! I've done it. Can I print again?'
Adult: 'Yes, of course.' (The printing procedure is repeated.)
D: 'Yehhh.' (Holds up the second printout proudly, then …) 'Do you want this? (Offers adult a plastic vegetable.)
Adult: 'Oh, thank you.'
D: (Produces a story book.) 'Will you read me this now?'

Figure 8

Age: Nursery
Location: ICT area
Activity: Using graphics software

Child M had been drawing pictures of Rosie (from 'Rosie and Jim') in the nursery on several occasions, in some cases working independently for as long as 30 minutes on the task. Noticing this his class teacher asked him if he would like to draw a picture of Rosie using the computer. M nodded enthusiastically but said, 'How?'. The teacher and the child moved into the computer area and the teacher introduced M to the 'Dazzle' painting/drawing software. M was very clear about the picture he wished to produce and the colours he would need.
M: 'Rosie needs red ties on her shoes.'
The teacher guided him in colour selection, clicking with the mouse and editing his drawing. By the end of the activity M was able to select his own colours from the menu, and was thrilled with the finished picture.

Figure 9

Age: Nursery
Location: Outside visit/Small world play
Activity: ICT in the wider world, visiting the traffic lights

A group of nursery children visited the local crossing point as part of a walk around the local area. At the road junction staff discussed road safety and the operation of the pelican crossing. The children experienced operating the lights, waiting for vehicles to stop and crossing the road in an orderly fashion with an adult. Back in the nursery a floor mat showing roads and buildings was set out with a number of toy vehicles and a petrol station. A classroom helper made a battery powered set of traffic lights operated by simple rocker switches. The children were able to switch the red, amber and green lights on and off in sequence. The adult helper worked with a group of children to show them how to operate the switches, to model the sequence, to elicit information from the children about the meaning of the lights based on their visit and to encourage turn taking and sharing.

Adult: 'Did you go to see the traffic lights yesterday?'
A and C: 'Yes.'
B: 'And we pushed the button.'
Adult: 'Oh did you. What happened?'
B: 'We crossed the road.'
Adult: 'Ahhh, well can you see what I've got here?'
C: (Picks up traffic lights.) 'It looks like a doggy!'
Adult: (Smiling) 'Yes it does a bit doesn't it. Those are its legs and that's its head. Does anyone else know what it is?'
B: 'It's got lights.'
Adult: 'That's right, they're traffic lights like the ones you went to see.' (Switches on Stop light.) 'What colour is the light?'
A: 'Red!'
Adult: 'That's right, well done. What do the cars have to do when the light is red?'
C: 'Stop!'
Adult: 'Yes they do.'
D: 'My dad stops when it goes red.'
Adult: 'That's good, so do I. What colour is this light then?'
A, B and C: 'Yellow!'

D: 'Orange!'
Adult: 'Yes, it's orangy yellow. What do the cars do when the light is orangy yellow?'
D, A and C: 'GO!'
Adult: 'Oh nearly, it means get ready doesn't it. And what colour is this light?'
A,B,C and D: 'Green!'
Adult: 'Well done, you know your colours don't you. What does the green light mean?'
A,B,C,D: 'GO!'
The adult facilitates the play as the children line up cars and toy people and take it in turns to operate the lights. Child B begins to take a lead in organising the play and the players.
B: (Switches on the green light.) 'Go on! Go on!' (C moves a toy lorry around the mat as instructed.)
B to Adult: 'You be that one.' (Hands over a toy car.)
After a few minutes B moves away to the quiet reading area.
C and A both move to take charge of the traffic lights.
C gets there first, grabs the lights and clutches them proprietarily to his chest. (To Adult and A.) 'We're supposed to share in nursery aren't we!'

Figure 10

The learning environment can have a significant impact upon young children's progress and development. An environment that stimulates the children, that is accessible to them and that contains high quality resources is more likely to support and encourage learning. For the purposes of this section the term 'learning environment' will include ICT resources and the physical surroundings, indoor and outdoor. The most valuable resource of all, the adults, are dealt with separately in the section on the role of the practitioner (p. 63). This section will consider ways of creating a learning environment to support children's learning about and through ICT by making the best possible use of the space and equipment available and by planning for ICT.

Planning the curriculum

Good early years practitioners are able to spot opportunities to capitalise on children's interests and enthusiasms as in Figure 9 and this skill is underpinned by their ability to plan for children's learning. Planning for ICT in the early years ought to be indistinguishable from planning for any other aspect of the early years curriculum in that it ought to seek to provide opportunities for play and for dialogue with peers and adults (Sharp *et al.* 2000). Practitioners need to consider ways in which ICT can be incorporated into existing provision to extend and enhance learning rather than seeing ICT as simply a series of free-standing computer based drill and skill activities separate from the rest of the provision.

Early years planning should show where continuity and progression exist in the provision for ICT. Continuity describes those aspects of a child's experiences that stay the same irrespective of their age; in other words significant features of ICT that occur on a regular basis throughout a child's time in nursery and reception settings. Some examples of continuity relating to ICT in the early years are listed below.

+ Encouraging children to use the correct terminology when talking about their work with

ICT, for example *dial, rewind, eject, keyboard, monitor, menu, font, printer or icon*;

♦ Providing regular and frequent opportunities to use the technology to increase skills and confidence;

♦ Encouraging younger children to work in pairs on the computer to foster co-operative and collaborative work as well as communication, language and literacy skills. Some research (Weeks 2000) has suggested, for example, that more than two young children in front of a PC screen may result in some redundancy;

♦ Ensuring experience of a wide and varied range of ICT equipment and skills throughout the children's time in nursery and reception. This includes using programmable toys/vehicles, listening stations, musical keyboards and real world applications as well as computer keyboards, operating the mouse, printing out work, saving work and using a range of word processing, graphics and data handling software;

♦ Using ICT in both indoor and outdoor contexts.

Progression sets out how children's learning is expected to advance during their time in nursery and reception in terms of the acquisition of knowledge and skills and the development of understanding, values and attitudes (Figure 11). The content and sequence of learning activities are structured through long, medium and short term planning, and practitioners monitor and assess children's progress in order to match new tasks to their developing capabilities to enable them to make further progress. Bruner's notion of a *spiral curriculum* offers a useful model of progression (Wood 1998). Children revisit key elements of the early years ICT curriculum throughout their nursery and reception experience (continuity), and each time it is at a higher level of understanding or refinement (progression).

Progression in ICT	Examples
Showing an interest in ICT	Asking/learning about the uses of ICT around the nursery/school (for example, fax, phone, photocopiers) Asking/learning about the uses of ICT in the world (for example, vending machines, databases, barcode readers, mobile phones) Playing with ICT in the home (for example, battery operated/programmable toys)
Operating simple equipment	Using the tape recorder/listening station to listen to taped stories and music Asking/learning about switching on and closing down procedures for the PC Incorporating ICT into role play situations Operating the pelican crossing during an out of school visit Knowing the names of examples of ICT (for example, computer, mobile)

Progression in ICT	Examples
Performing simple functions	Rewinding, fast forwarding and ejecting tapes Taping and playing back own stories or music Using letter keys, Delete and spacebar on the PC Programming the Roamer or Pixie to follow a route Using the mouse/arrow keys to select items on a computer screen (clicking/double clicking) Extending technical vocabulary
Recognising everyday applications and using ICT to support learning (QCA 2000: 92)	Printing out and saving work on the PC and changing colour or pen width using a painting and drawing package with help Navigating CD-ROM materials including non-fiction and talking stories Sharing ICT skills and knowledge with peers

Figure 11

Figures 12 and 13 offer examples of medium and short-term planning involving the use of ICT in nursery and reception settings.

Using ICT in and out of the setting

Depending on the ICT in question some activities may be largely static and located in a specific ICT area, such as using the painting and drawing package on the PC in Figure 9. Other ICT resources may best be deployed outside any designated ICT

Reception		Half term	HT 1	HT 2	HT 3	HT 4	HT 5	HT 6
Area of Learning: Creative Development				Main Theme: Festivals and Celebrations				
Activity	Learning objectives (Early Learning Goals)	Monitoring and assessment		Resources		Links to other areas of learning		
Making Diva lamps for Divali	Exploring shape and form in 3D	• make 3D structures • make constructions		Plasticine, clay, play dough, pictures of Diva lamps		PSE and K&U – awareness and interest in different cultures and beliefs PD – explore malleable materials		
Making Divali patterns (rangoli) using coloured shapes and acetates on the light table/OHP	Exploring shape and form in 2D	• begin to differentiate colours • choosing colours for a purpose		Light table, *OHP, internet pictures of rangoli patterns,* coloured acetate shapes		K&U – commenting on patterns, *operating equipment* PD – manipulate materials to achieve planned effect		

Figure 12

Reception		Half term	HT 1	HT 2	HT 3	HT 4	HT 5	HT 6
Area of Learning: Creative Development								
				Main Theme: Festivals and Celebrations				
Activity	Learning objectives (Early Learning Goals)	Monitoring and assessment		Resources		Links to other areas of learning		
Bonfire night paintings	Exploring colour, texture and shape in 2D	• using senses to explore texture • begin to describe texture • understand different media can be combined • experiment to create different textures		Black paper, glitter, glue, sequins, coloured metallic paper, thick paints		PSE – show care and concern for self (i.e. dangers of fireworks) PD – hand-eye co-ordination, increasing manipulative control, using simple tools		
Listening to music in festivals and celebrations	Matching movements to music	• responding to sound with body movement • imitate/create movement in response to music • begin to move rhythmically		*Listening station/ tape player, CD player*		PD – responding to rhythm, moving with confidence and imagination *K&U – operating equipment*		

Figure 12 *continued*

Activity	Learning objectives (Early Learning Goals)	Monitoring and assessment	Resources	Links to other areas of learning
Making bonfire night music	Explore different sounds Changing sounds	• using representation as a means of communication • capturing experiences with music • expressing and communicating ideas, thoughts and feelings	Shakers, triangles, cymbals, drums, chime bars, guitars, *electronic keyboard*	PD – hand-eye co-ordination, increasing manipulative control, using simple tools K&U – *operating equipment*
Role Play Area – The Card Shop, making and selling greetings cards for different festivals and celebrations	Using imagination in role-play	• use resources to support role-play • engage in imaginative play based on own experiences • play co-operatively and act out a narrative	Paper, card, mark making equipment (felt pens, colouring crayons), envelopes, *PC drawing package, electronic till*	PSE – working as part of a group, sharing and taking turns K&U – *operating equipment, performing simple functions* CLL – initiate conversation

Figure 12 *continued*

CLL = Communication, language and literacy. K&U = Knowledge and understanding of the world. PD = Physical development. PSE = Personal, social, emotional development

51

Nursery session planner	
Learning objectives (Early Learning Goals)	**Activity**
• Counting/Use everyday words to describe position and/or distance such as *further/nearer* (Mathematical Development) • Using ICT to support their learning (Knowledge and Understanding of the world)	Small group work. Practising language related to position and distance. Introduce the Pixie. Programme the vehicle to navigate its way to people and pictures.
	Resources
	Pixie, floor mat/grid, small world figures, animal pictures, ball
Introduction	• practise rolling the ball between group members • introduce key words/phrases – forwards, backwards, in front, behind, further, nearer, longer, shorter, next to
Development	• introduce the Pixie • send the Pixie to a child • children to take turns programming the vehicle to send it to their peers. Discuss programming sequence and relationship between distance and number of forward commands • introduce the floor mat/grid with farmyard animal pictures in different cells and matching small world play figures. Remind the children of the previous week's visit to the farm

Figure 13

	• who can find a picture of a lamb? Who thinks they can get the Pixie to take the lamb to the picture? How will you get there? Repeat with other animals. Encourage use of mathematical language
Differentiation	• more able = more distant picture/more complicated route
Extension activities/Links	• knowledge and Understanding of the world – small world play 'The Farm'
Monitoring and assessment	• offer solutions to problems (Math. development: 76) • instructing a programmable toy (Math. development: 80) • operate simple equipment (K&U: 92) • perform simple functions using ICT (K&U: 92)

Figure 13 *continued*

area, such as locating the keyboard on the music table, placing the listening station/tape player in the quiet corner or placing ICT resources in the role-play area as in Figure 8. Even non-functional equipment can serve a purpose in early years settings as was shown earlier (p. 25) when an obsolete and non-functioning PC still proved useful as a stimulus for imaginative play. Labelling ICT resources within the nursery or classroom may help children to become familiar with words like *telephone, computer, printer, camera* or *mouse* and displaying work relating to ICT, possibly in and around a designated ICT area is one way of valuing the children's efforts. The nursery planning sheet shown in Figure 4 (p. 2) includes the displaying of photographs taken using a digital camera, other examples might include a gallery of colour printouts of children's artwork using painting and drawing software.

Some activities involving ICT may be more fluid and require more space. As with other aspects of the early years curriculum the learning environment includes the outdoor as well as the indoor areas. As Edgington makes clear (2002) *'There's no such thing as bad weather, only unsuitable clothing.'* There is no reason to confine work with ICT to the indoor areas alone. Digital cameras, walkie-talkies, programmable and remote controlled vehicles, tape recorders and laptop computers all lend themselves to use in outdoor environments. In Figure 5 (p. 23) the adult helper underestimated the short-term impact of introducing the equipment and the danger of the activity disrupting other children in the vicinity. With hindsight they realised that this was an ICT task much better suited to the outdoor area and this is where it subsequently ended up. Limited conceptions of ICT that focus largely on trolley bound PCs make it easy to forget the opportunities that exist to extend learning beyond the classroom environment. Although the limitations on moving a PC on a trolley into the great outdoors are obvious, there is plenty of scope to take all manner of other ICT resources into the outdoor area quickly and easily. Indeed in some cases ICT may be better suited to the outdoor environment with its greater space and capacity to absorb noise and movement.

Identifying and accessing ICT resources beyond the classroom is one way of helping children to see ICT being used in real contexts, for example taking children to the nursery or school office to send a fax or use the photocopier. In Figure 8 the power lead was removed from the photocopier in the role-play area in the interests of health and safety and concerns about children looking directly into the bright lights. Children were taken to the nursery office to use another photocopier and drew on the experience in their role-play. ICT resources may also be present in off-site activities, for example pointing out the concept keyboard in the grocery store and talking to the children about its use. Many young children may have the opportunity to visit the local hospital with their parents when another sibling is on the way, they may observe the ultrasound scanning machine in operation and return to the nursery/classroom with a printout of the image. In Figure 10 the children gained an understanding of the operation of the pelican crossing technology which they were able to make use of subsequently in their small world play back in the nursery.

Organizing and managing the computer(s)

Although ICT is composed of much more than just computers, the use of PCs in early years learning environments does raise some specific organizational issues for practitioners to consider. Consequently some specific commentary concerning computers is offered below.

Hardware

Where the ICT resource being organised is a computer, practitioners may wish to give particular attention to the following questions:

+ Where are the plug sockets? Do you really want extension cables and wires running across the floor?

+ Do you have a good line of sight to the computer so that you can see if and when you need to intervene to support learning or to ensure equality of opportunity?

+ Is the computer screen set at an appropriate height for young children or are they forced to lean their heads back at an awkward angle? Does the screen face away from the windows or do the children have to squint through the reflected glare?

- How well do the children cope with the mouse? Do they know which button to click or double click? A coloured sticker on the left-hand mouse button may serve as a useful reminder. Small hands may struggle with equipment designed for adults and it is possible to purchase a special child sized mouse.

- Are other peripherals and resources to hand or do the children have to wander around the nursery/classroom to locate them?

- Would it be useful to invest in a lower case keyboard to lay over the existing capitals?

- Is it better for children to experience computer use in the nursery/classroom as part of their everyday activities or should they go to a separate ICT suite? In addition to pedagogical concerns about how young children learn best (Caruso Davis and Shade 1994; Siraj-Blatchford and Siraj-Blatchford 2001) there are also practical considerations; just imagine the staffing implications of thirty 4- and 5-year-olds all encountering the need for adult support and input simultaneously.

- How long should young children spend in front of a computer at any one time? Some research has suggested that most young children left to their own devices do not want to spend long periods in front of a computer screen and are more likely to use the technology for short periods before opting to move on to other activities (Pierce 1994). Child D in Figure 8 is a good illustration of this. Siraj-Blatchford and Siraj-

Blatchford (2002) recommend an average of 10–20 minutes for nursery aged children in the interests of health and safety with occasional provision made for longer periods where children are particularly engrossed in an activity.

Software

Much of the software available to early years practitioners can be categorised as either *generic* (open-ended) software or *content rich* software (Sharp *et al.* 2000). In some cases, for example certain graphics and music applications, the software incorporates elements of both categories (Sharp *et al.* 2000). Generic or open-ended software is not specifically related to any particular topic, but can be used to extend and enhance children's efforts to communicate and handle information across a wide range of activities. Generic software, such as word processors, databases, graphics packages, or music CD-ROMs, has the potential to empower the user by freeing her/him from some of the more mundane, mechanical or routine aspects of an activity, thus enabling her/him to engage in higher order thinking and problem solving skills. Editing and redrafting benefit in particular from the use of open-ended software. Using drawing or painting packages as in Figure 9 offers advantages for children in terms of the quality of the finish and the opportunity to adjust their artwork in a way that does not require excessive use of materials or messy outcomes (HMI/DES 1991).

Content rich software packages can constitute powerful tools for children. CD-ROM talking books, electronic encyclopaedias and computer games or simulations can all offer opportunities for exploration and discovery in which the user is being both active and interactive. Software of this sort may encourage young children's disposition to be curious and to want to find out. At the same time, setting any problems or challenges in meaningful, familiar or relevant contexts, may lend itself to the promotion of collaborative work and discussion. This said, such software ought to be considered as additional and *supplementary* to first-hand experience rather than as a replacement for it (NAEYC 1996). Furthermore, some content rich software is essentially instructional in nature with the computer acting as a teacher. While there may be a place for this type of software it is not without its problems and limitations, and these have been pointed out at length by the United States' Alliance for Childhood (2000). Some of these packages are premised on the belief that skills and knowledge can be reduced to, and learnt as, a set of discrete chunks of information such as word and letter recognition or addition and subtraction tasks. However, isolated skills and knowledge learned in drill and skill activities may not bear much relation to the use of the same skills and knowledge in contexts where they are employed for a real purpose. Such packages frequently incorporate an essentially behaviourist approach to learning in which rewards such as flashing screens and jingles are assumed to improve young children's learning by reinforcing the correct responses. Many early years researchers and practitioners would not share this assumption about young children as learners (Siraj-Blatchford and Siraj-Blatchford 2002). The fact that software is content rich in no way obviates the need for adult intervention to help the children get the most out of it in terms of learning *through* ICT and learning *about* ICT.

Early years practitioners therefore need to exercise their own professional judgement when it comes to choosing software packages. While they offer the opportunity to introduce a range of tools into the classroom that are potentially powerful and/or liberating in nature (Sharp *et al.* 2000: 7), a brief glance at educational resources catalogues makes clear the enormous range of software available to early years practitioners and some packages will be more appropriate than others. The challenge for practitioners is to establish which software is most appropriate for their children. A number of organizations offer advice to practitioners and others on the strengths and weaknesses of different software packages:

♦ Teachers Evaluating Educational Multimedia (TEEM) (www.teem.org.uk/) provides practitioners with access to evaluations of educational multimedia written by classroom teachers;

♦ The British Educational Communications and Technology Agency (BECTa) (www.becta.org.uk) offers practitioners an ICT advice service (www.ictadvice.org.uk) as well as access to an educational software database;

♦ The Parents Information Network (www.pin.org.uk) provides software evaluations as well as advice on a wide range of ICT matters including health and safety;

♦ Micros and Primary Education (MAPE) (www.mape.org.uk) offers practitioners advice on and links to software evaluation and suggestions for using ICT in the different areas of learning to be found in the Curriculum guidance for the foundation stage (QCA 2000).

When considering which software to make available in the nursery or reception class practitioners may wish to visit one or more of the web addresses above and at the same time ask themselves the following questions:

♦ Will the software support the learning/ educational objectives?

♦ Is any content provided accurate and *inclusive* in its design? Alternatively is the content partisan in its focus or does it include unsuitable (for example, violent) material and perpetuate stereotypical images relating to gender, language, culture or socio-economic class? (Sharp *et al.* 2000)

♦ How easy is it for children and practitioners to use? Is it *transparent*? (Siraj-Blatchford and Siraj-Blatchford, 2002) Is it clear what the buttons, icons and menus are for? With content rich software is the information organised in such a way as to make *navigation* easy?

♦ Does the software provide useful support for practitioners, for example, a manual, on-screen help or a teachers page? (Sharp *et al.* 2000)

ICT in the Early Years

The internet

The internet can be a source of some concern for practitioners, particularly in relation to exposing young children to inappropriate subject matter. The lack of editorial control means that many websites are of low quality or are not suitable for direct use by children as a result of the level at which the text is written. Furthermore it is hard to imagine very young children navigating their way round a virtual environment in any meaningful way without adult support; practitioners ought to bear in mind NAEYC's comment on possible disparities between skills and comprehension (1996). This said, there is a great deal of material that practitioners can access on behalf of the children. Reputable organizations such as the BBC (www.bbc.co.uk/education) provide an immense amount of written and visual material of potential use to early years practitioners. Similarly, some schools and nurseries have created their own websites which can offer users an insight into practice with ICT in other early years settings. Guidance on using the internet with young children, in the home or in the nursery/school can be located on both the NAEYC and BECTa websites (www.naeyc.org; www.ictadvice.org.uk).

The Role of the Practitioner in
Teaching *about* and *through* ICT

Examples

Age: Reception
Location: Socio-dramatic role play area
Activity: CCTV in the Seaside Café and Shop

At lunchtime a video camera connected to an old portable television was set up in the Seaside Café and Shop. The shop already contained a toy electronic cash till, two pocket calculators and a telephone. On the monitor at the back of the shop the children could observe anyone entering the café/shop. The class teacher and other adults decided not to alert the children to the presence of the home made CCTV system initially in order to surprise them, generate a sense of excitement, awe and wonder and to observe the children's reactions.

As the children come in from the playground, most go and sit down on the carpet ready for registration. Two children (A & B) spot the video camera on its stand and wander over to look at it curiously. Another child (C) notices that there is something else in the corner. She walks over and finds the monitor.
C to A and B: 'Ahhh! I can see you!'
A and B rush over to the monitor.
A: 'Ah ha. You can see things.'
B calls to some of the other children to come and see and a small crowd forms with individuals taking turns to go into the camera's line of sight while the other children laugh as their image appears on the monitor.
The class teacher and another adult appear, smiling, and lead the children back to the carpet. The class teacher explains to the

children that she will tell them all about it after register. Once registration is over the class teacher explains that there is something new in the Seaside Café and Shop area. She tells the children that it's a video camera and asks them if they know why it's there. A few hands shoot up.

Class teacher: 'Yes E?'

E: 'It's for catching people who are stealing.'

Class teacher: 'That's right. In lots of shops they have cameras so that they can make sure people don't take things without paying for them.'

F: 'My daddy told me if you're naughty they catch you and call the police!'

Class teacher: 'That's right F they would call the police if someone was taking anything.'

G: 'Miss! Miss!'

Class teacher: 'Yes G?'

G: 'I went to Tesco's.'

Class teacher: 'Oh, did you? And did they have any cameras in the supermarket?'

G: (Nods solemnly.)

Class teacher: 'I thought they might. Thank you G. Well, anyway we've got the camera for the next few weeks so when it's your turn to play in the Seaside Café you'll be able to see what's going on in the shop. Now lets see what we're doing this afternoon ...'

Figure 14

Age: Reception
Location: Carpeted area
Activity: Audio/visual technologies in the Karaoke concert

The school was holding a Japanese week to coincide with the football World Cup. Parents who had visited or lived in Japan donated a range of artefacts from crockery and chopsticks to photographs, coins and even a wedding kimono. Staff in the reception class decided to hold a Karaoke session on the Thursday afternoon. At the beginning of the week the class teacher explained that Karaoke was a popular Japanese pastime. Some of the children were already familiar with the concept from discussions with older family members. The children were told that anyone who wanted to could sing a song and that they could do so with a friend if they would prefer. The majority of the children were keen to have a go and practised their songs at home during the following days. A small group with an adult helper constructed a low stage out of the wooden construction blocks. The video camera from Figure 14 was set up to film the performances and a working amplifier and microphone were also provided for the singers.

The day before the concert the class teacher offered the children a chance to practise their songs and learn how to operate the microphone.

Class teacher: 'Does anyone need to practise before tomorrow?' (A forest of hands appears.)

H: 'Mrs B, me and P HAVE GOT TO!'

Class teacher: (Laughing) 'Oh well we better make sure you get the chance then, hadn't we.'

Later …

Class teacher: 'Does anyone else have a song they'd like to practise?'

A: 'I've got one!'

Class teacher: 'Oh A, good. Up you come then.'

A: (Climbs onto the stage, holds microphone and strokes his chin thoughtfully.) 'Urm, how do you sing it again?'

On the day of the Karaoke concert many of the children brought costumes. A volunteer helper operated the CD player, introduced the *artists* and led the applause. Those children who did not want to sing were offered the chance to operate the video camera, supported by the class teacher, while another helper gave them the chance to take photographs using the digital camera. The tunes ranged from 'How Much is that Doggy in the Window', 'Twinkle Twinkle Little Star' and 'Bob the Builder', to modern pop songs from groups and individuals such as U2, S Club 7 and Kylie Minogue.

When the singing was over the children watched the concert played back on the TV monitor. The video was subsequently used during a parents' evening as an example of the work the children had been doing. It proved extremely popular and copies were requested.

Figure 15

Age: Nursery
Location: Quiet room
Activity: Operating the Pixie programmable vehicle

The class teacher and a classroom helper are working with a group of children in the quiet room. They are sitting in a rough circle and begin by naming a group member and rolling a ball to that person. The class teacher engages the children in discussion about who has not had a go and who is closer or further away. The class teacher then introduces the Pixie programmable vehicle. The classroom helper models the sequence of instruction for the children: *clear memory, forward button, go*. The classroom helper then names a child and instructs the Pixie to travel across the carpet to that child. The children smile and giggle as the vehicle trundles across the carpet, one clutches himself in excitement. The class teacher helps the recipient of the Pixie to decide who to send it to next, talks to the child about the comparative distances involved and asks the child to suggest how many forward commands will be necessary to get the vehicle to travel the required distance. The other children join in enthusiastically with suggestions. All the children are offered the chance to have repeated attempts. Whenever the vehicle stops short the children are encouraged to see if they can correct the shortfall by reprogramming the vehicle to travel the remaining distance. The class teacher then introduces a board with some pictures of farm animals on. She talks to the children about their recent visit to the farm and the children are encouraged to name the animals and talk about their experiences. The class teacher produces some model animals that match the pictures and asks the children if they think they can give the animals a ride to the correct picture. The children respond eagerly and take it in turns to place an animal on top of the vehicle and programme it. Although this is the first time the children have encountered the Pixie some of them prove surprisingly adept at remembering the programming sequence required and demonstrate considerable skill in gauging the number of forward commands necessary to reach their chosen destination. The class teacher decides to offer the children further play opportunities during the following week to give them an opportunity to reinforce their learning and to introduce them to the *turn right* and *turn left* buttons.

Figure 16

The Role of the Practitioner in Teaching

Perhaps the most valuable resources in this, as in all aspects of early years education, are the practitioners and other responsible adults. High adult:child ratios help to make the most effective use of materials and equipment and ensure that children get the encouragement and guidance they need to make progress. A great deal has been written about the important role that practitioners and other adults can make in supporting young children's learning and development (Marsh 1994; Bruce 1997; QCA 2000; Keenan 2002; Merry 2002). At the same time, inspection and other evidence (Haughton 2000; Siraj-Blatchford *et al.* 2002; Moyles *et al.* 2002) seems to suggest that in some settings at least, the need for *participatory interaction and assisted performance* (Meade 2000), often so much in evidence in early years education, may not always be translated into practice where the use of ICT is concerned. To be effective ICT needs to be integrated appropriately into the early years curriculum. Trooping whole classes to designated ICT suites, for example, may result in ICT experiences that are inappropriate given the ways in which young children learn. There may be practical difficulties in terms of staffing and young children may spend far longer in front of a computer screen than is advisable from a health and safety point of view (Pierce 1994; Caruso Davis and Shade 1994; Siraj-Blatchford and Siraj-Blatchford 2002). Equally, unsupported involvement in the nursery/classroom with unsuitable or undemanding drill and skill software packages is unlikely to provide much in the way of intellectual and creative challenge for children (Edgington 1998).

The role of the early years educator in promoting children's learning and development has a number of interrelated dimensions. Practitioners need to plan and provide an interesting and stimulating learning environment for children. They need to monitor children's progress and needs. They need to intervene sensitively in children's play to support and extend learning, as well as knowing when to stand back. They need to provide emotional support for children, acknowledging their efforts and praising their achievements. They need to challenge children to try new things, take risks and attain new levels of achievement. Jones and Reynolds (1992 in DECS 1996) identified a number of components to the role of the early years practitioner:

◆ The practitioner as **planner** – ensuring a programme in which play is a priority, including providing a range of different play spaces;

◆ The practitioner as **stage manager** – setting up the physical environment to facilitate children's play including the provision of props and resources, as well as time to explore and develop ideas;

◆ The practitioner as **mediator** – mediating between children and mediating between the physical environment and the children, assisting children in their play by modelling and explaining problem solving skills which children can practise on their own;

- The practitioner as **player** – actively participating in children's play as a co-player, offering ideas and knowledge to help children sustain and extend their play;

- The practitioner as **scribe** – collecting, organising and recording data on the content/quality of children's play;

- The practitioner as **assessor and communicator** – using observations to make judgements about children's development. These judgements then inform decision making about future practice and provide a basis for communication with and reporting to parents.

(DECS 1996)

Planning and stage managing

If Jones and Reynolds' model is applied to the use of ICT in the early years then planning ought to show where and how new technologies can be incorporated into the learning program. Figure 17 below shows the nursery planning for the imaginative play area from Figure 8 in which the ICT elements are clearly identifiable.

The props and resources available to the children should include as broad a range of ICT equipment as possible (Figure 18). In some cases the resources may be freely available to the children, in others they may require adults to mediate and assist in the operation of the technology. In some instances these props and resources may be permanently available, for example tape recorders/

Role-play area – The Office

Resources
- Photocopier
- Computer and printer
- Telephone
- Dictaphone/tape recorder
- Calculator
- OHP
- Notice board
- Calendar
- Diaries
- Mark making materials (pens, pencils, paper)
- Envelopes
- Clock
- ID tags/badges

Roles (Children)
- Office clerk
- School secretary
- Customer relations
- Manager

Roles (Teacher/adults)
- Customer
- Worker
- 'Boss'

Story lines
- Answering the phone/ making appointments
- Writing letters
- Organising presents for Father Christmas

Key questions
- Who are you writing to?
- Can I make an appointment?
- What time/day can I come?
- How does it work?

Opportunities for learning
- Acting out office worker roles
- Become familiar with office technology
- Operating technology (switching on and off, using a keyboard, printing out)
- Writing for a purpose
- Encountering new language/vocabulary

Learning objectives
- Personal/social development – sharing and taking turns
- Communication, language and literacy – talking with peers and adults; writing for a purpose
- Knowledge and understanding of the world – operating equipment; performing simple functions; recognising everyday uses of ICT

Figure 17

listening stations in the quiet area, electronic tills and calculators in the role-play shop or familiar software packages on the computer. In other cases the experience of ICT might revolve around a specific event or theme. In the nursery, photographs of the children were taken using a digital camera as part of some work on *Ourselves and our families*. These were then displayed alongside photographs brought from home showing the children as babies (Figure 4, p. 21). In addition, nursery staff encouraged some children to answer the telephone under adult supervision to foster social and communication skills as well as offering hands on experience with another aspect of ICT. Practitioners can also capitalise on examples of ICT in the world outside nursery or school during visits, such as supermarket barcodes, patient databases at the vets or the pelican crossing featured in Figure 10 (p. 43).

Mediating and playing

As mediator and player the practitioner ensures that children learning about or through ICT are eligible for the same quality intervention and support that they would receive if they were involved in any other activity, whether it is small world play, mark making at the writing table, or building a tower with the construction materials. The technology alone cannot be assumed to be doing the teaching. First-hand experience is only part of the equation, quality interactions with peers and adults are a vital

The practitioner as stage manager: Thinking about possible ICT props and resources	
Digital camera	Programmable/remote controlled toys including Roamer/Pixie
Scanner	Electronic toy cash register
Fax machine	Walkie-talkies
Telephone/Mobile	Radio/CD player
Photocopier	Electronic calculator
Concept keyboard	Personal organiser
Overhead projector	Computer
Tape recorder/player	CD-ROM
Television	Internet/World Wide Web
Electronic keyboard (musical)/music mat/battery operated instruments	Programmable consumer durables (video player, microwave, washing machine)
Video camera	Electronic whiteboard

Figure 18

concomitant if progress and learning is to take place. Sayeed and Guerin (2000) describe this kind of quality intervention whereby an adult and child interact in relation to an activity as a *mediated learning experience* (MLE). They state that without MLEs a child's social and academic achievement can be hindered, whilst with them practitioners can go some way towards ameliorating any inequalities in terms of social, cultural, or economic back-grounds. When engaged in an MLE the practitioner adapts the *frequency, order, content, location and intensity of the activity* based on her/his assessment of the child's needs.

> 'The adult arouses care, curiosity and alertness in the child and helps the child to understand the activity so that they can be successful in it.'
>
> (Sayeed and Guerin 2000: 80)

In Figure 5 (p. 23) the adult encouraged the children to play and work co-operatively, sharing the resources, taking turns and working with others less confident than themselves. Children's ideas were respected and supported including the relocation of the activity to a larger outdoor space. Children without previous experience were helped by being offered technical advice and the child who was uncertain was allowed time and space to build up her confidence. Similarly in Figure 16 the class teacher used her knowledge and understanding of the children's capabilities as well as her ongoing observations during the session to judge the level of challenge presented to each child and the degree of guidance provided.

One factor to consider when mediating learning for children involving ICT is how the technology will be introduced. One option is for practitioners to model the use of a piece of technology with individuals and small groups of children at a point of need. In Figure 14 once the children had been directed to various areas for the afternoon session a classroom helper joined the group in the role-play area to introduce the group to the video camera and monitor. Similarly in Figure 16 the class teacher and a classroom helper worked closely with the group of nursery children using this approach. Although of high relevance for the children concerned and offering instant feedback, the approach can be problematic in settings where there may be 25 other children in the class and non-teaching support is intermittent or unavailable.

Introducing new technology to larger groups or the whole class and allowing children to rotate around the activity during the day or week is a second option. In Figure 15 the whole class was shown the amplifier and microphone in this way. However, with large groups it can be hard for all the children to observe such an introduction clearly, particularly where the technology involved is more complicated such as computer software. Unless the technology involved is reasonably simple to use, *transparent* (Siraj-Blatchford and Siraj-Blatchford 2002), and children are able to use it fairly quickly as they were in Figure 15 they may not remember much of the introduction.

A third option is for practitioners to encourage children to disseminate their ICT expertise to other children in the nursery/classroom. Cascading their skills and knowledge to their peers in this way could be seen as an example of children scaffolding the learning of others. It certainly appears attractive as an efficient approach, however it does require careful monitoring of the group dynamics to ensure that any children being *taught* by their peers are actually gaining access to the technology and are learning. While grouping in this way can be useful there can also be a tendency for the more able, confident or experienced to monopolise the activity, as in Figure 7 (p. 36), and practitioners must be ready to step in and intervene if necessary. It is easy to be seduced on occasion by the quality of the resource and the obvious enthusiasm of some pupils, but the need to monitor and ensure quality in teaching and learning, not least in terms of equality of opportunity, is a key feature of the practitioner's role. Young children's technical *know how* may be well in advance of their social skills and practitioners need to watch out for children who:

♦ Dominate an activity by making unilateral decisions;

♦ Monopolise the equipment;

♦ Tell other children what to do in a bossy manner leading to squabbles and bickering;

♦ Are being excluded by other children who ignore their ideas and contributions irrespective of whether they prove to be right or wrong;

♦ Are struggling to operate the technology;

♦ Do not appear to understand the nature of the task.

None of the potential of ICT to extend and enhance learning is inevitable and seems unlikely without sensitive and informed mediation at times on the part of practitioners. Without such intervention the use of ICT could just as easily result in individual children taking over while their less assertive or knowledgeable peers accede to the demands of the more dominant without discussion. Such a situation can result in choices and decisions being made without any apparent thought or consideration of alternatives. Dispute and inequality can become the distinguishing features of children's ICT experiences where high quality adult involvement is lacking; in this respect ICT is no different to any other aspect of the early years learning environment. The adult plays a crucial role in mediating between the children themselves as well as between the environment and the child (Sayeed and Guerin 2000). Careful thought about grouping and offering open access does not guarantee equal participation. Groupings and pairings may need to be altered in the light of experience, and children who appear reluctant or intimidated by the technology encouraged sensitively, as in Figure 5 (p. 23), to have a go. By observing children soon after they have started an activity involving ICT, there is still time to intervene at an early stage if practitioners become aware of unrest or unacceptable behaviour leading to the exclusion of certain children.

Scribing, monitoring and assessing

Practitioners need to look for evidence of progression in young children's learning about and through ICT in a number of areas.

◆ Skills in ICT. For example, operating the *play, pause, fast forward* and *rewind* buttons on the listening station, or using the mouse, Delete key, saving and printing work using the computer.

The Role of the Practitioner in Teaching

- Knowledge and understanding of ICT. For example, awareness of the advantages of ICT (for example, speed, quality, editing/redrafting, interactivity); when its use is and is not warranted; familiarity with types and uses of ICT in the world around them and experience of using a range of ICT equipment to communicate information, handle information and to control systems.

- Attitudes and dispositions towards ICT. For example, displaying an interest in and curiosity about the technology, co-operating with peers and adults, sharing ideas, equipment and information.

It seems likely that children's learning *about* ICT may be easier to evidence than their learning *through* ICT as causality will not always be clear. While there will be times when young children produce concrete evidence of their awareness and understanding in relation to ICT, as in Figure 19, many of the judgements made by practitioners about young children's learning and development will be based on observations. Practitioners constantly check on children's progress through classroom observations involving the whole class, groups and individuals. These observations, such as an overheard conversation between children, or being presented with a striking piece of art work, provide a means by which children's knowledge, skills and dispositions can be checked and explored and can help to define more clearly any individual contributions to a group task. They are an informal

Figure 19: Nursery picture of mobile phone

and integral part of work with young children, a natural part of the minute by minute interactions in the nursery or classroom and are essential for children's continuous assessment. In Figure 6 (p. 25) the adult was surprised at the level of ICT awareness demonstrated by Child A who was only 5 years old, including his awareness of faxes, and correct terminology such as *typing*, not writing. At the same time his final remarks showed that his understanding of the concept of *country* was still incomplete. As Edgington (1998) points out, ongoing and unplanned observations centre on those things which *draw themselves to the practitioner's attention*. While important, they do not necessarily offer a more rounded picture, they may for example fail to pick up the events that take place quietly (Edgington 1998: 127). While it is not possible to observe everything that goes on in a nursery or reception class, making use of more planned, targeted and focused observations may well serve to complement the unplanned, ongoing kind as well as sharpening a practitioner's skills in this area generally (Edgington 1998: 128). Focused observations may well challenge adult assumptions about children and their ICT capabilities because they offer information that might otherwise be missed. Some examples of nursery observations relating to ICT are set out in Figure 20.

As Sharman *et al.* (1995: 2) state, an observation is akin to a *camera shot*, while it does not lie, it can distort. Although the term observation suggests passivity on the part of the teacher, the reality is usually far more active and involves more than just sitting and watching. Practitioners often have to check their observations through careful questioning, discussion and further observations. Discussing activities with children as part of classroom observation is a very useful device for locating evidence of a child's success, diagnosing learning difficulties, monitoring progress over a period of time, and developing some insight into the ways in which a particular child learns and works. A child's initial response to questioning is not necessarily an accurate or reliable guide to knowledge and competence (SCAA 1997), similarly actions and behaviour can be misinterpreted. Consequently practitioners need to base their judgements and assessments about children's ICT

ICT in the Early Years

Showing an interest in ICT
A: (Pointing to the photocopier in the role-play area.) 'Why doesn't that work?'

Developing an understanding of how things work
B: (Watches a computer's start up procedure and points to the coloured bar showing how far advanced the procedure is.) 'When it gets right up t'top again it'll come on.'

Familiarity with some of the correct terminology and with some of the uses to which ICT can be put
C to Adult: 'You want to see on the computer, I've got a *folder*!'
Adult: 'Have you? On that computer?' (Points to the Nursery PC.)
C: 'No on my computer at home.'
Adult: 'Oh. What's in your folder?'
C: 'Woody.'
Adult: 'Woody?'
C: (Withering look.) 'Woody! Buzz Lightyear! Woody!'
Adult: 'Ohhh, I see! Buzz Lightyear's Woody.'
C: 'Yes, and I've got Monkey Island.'
Adult: (Baffled) 'Oh?' (Subsequent enquiry reveals Monkey Island to be a computer game played by one of the child's parents.)

D enters the nursery creative area carrying a mobile phone from the role-play area. She places it next to her on the table while she begins to paint. After a few minutes she picks up the phone and begins to press the buttons.
Adult: 'What are you doing D?'
D: 'I'm *texting* Julie.'
Adult: 'Oh, what's your message?'
D: 'To see if she can pick me up from nursery.'
D places the phone back on the table and starts painting again. A few minutes later she stops again, places the phone to her ear and starts talking.
D: 'Hello Julie, are you picking me up from nursery or is my mum?' (Pauses for the imaginary reply.) 'Oh, okay.'
D then returns to her painting.

Taking turns, sharing and showing concern for others
E to F: 'Can I have a go?'
F places ICT equipment out of reach of E.
G to F: 'Let him have it, he's only small.'

Figure 20

capabilities on more than one snapshot. The class teacher in Figure 16 for example was impressed by the apparent speed with which some of the children had developed a degree of competence with the Pixie. Consequently she planned further sessions to check on their understanding and to move their learning forward.

The value of observation conducted over a period of time was demonstrated in relation to Figure 14. A small group of children spent the first part of the afternoon in the Seaside Café and Shop and attention focused almost exclusively on the CCTV system. The children were very excited and not much buying and selling of drinks or seaside rock was taking place, let alone imaginative play incorporating the technology. Instead the children turned the monitor round so that they could *perform* (i.e. dancing and pulling funny faces) in front of the camera while simultaneously watching themselves on the monitor. Three weeks after the introduction of the CCTV system into the class shop, however, a classroom helper noticed a group of children playing in the role-play area. Three children were sitting in a row behind a table. A fourth child stood on a pedestal operating the video camera, lifting her head from the view finder from time to time to check the TV monitor. One of the children behind the desk grabbed a sheaf of papers and shuffled them meaningfully before looking into the camera and launching into an impromptu news bulletin in which England had won the World Cup with the winning goal scored by David Beckham. Once again the novelty had worn off; there were no excited dances and funny faces this time. This group at least were no longer dependent upon play scenarios set up by the adults, they were incorporating the technology into their own scenarios and setting their own agenda. Not only that, but they displayed a surprising level of knowledge and understanding about news broadcasts which no-one in the school had discussed with them.

When observation is the chosen method of assessment it is important to bear in mind that inappropriate approaches to the act of observing could affect the outcomes. Some children might seek to play to the gallery, while others may become shy or withdrawn, particularly if the technology is new and they have not yet had time to explore its use. Strategies for reducing the risks with young children include:

- Giving the children time for the novelty of new technology to wear off before making planned observations;

- Observing during participation in play activities and adopting the roles of *player and mediator* (Jones and Reynolds 1992 in DECS 1996) in which attempts to exert overt authority over children are not made. In other words, seeking the *attenuation of one's own authority* that is part and parcel of having adult status in the eyes of the children (Fine and Sandstrom in Holmes 1998);

- Paying close attention to non-verbal signals and the use of appropriate language. For example, using pupil furniture and equipment to get down to the children's level, or learning how children ask to join in with activities and imitating this;

- Talking to children in pairs or small groups which may be less threatening and allow children to sustain conversation for longer periods creating chances for peer interactions and fostering participation (Holmes 1998);

- Combining unrelated tasks (for example, drawing) with unstructured and informal discussions. As children tend to concentrate on the drawing they may be less likely to be distracted by events around them or to regard the discussion as intimidating (Holmes 1998);

- Expressing and demonstrating enjoyment of time spent with the children on ICT activities and offering praise, recognition and respect for their ideas and contributions when using the technology.

A single practitioner cannot realistically expect to gather assessment evidence on large numbers of children simultaneously through observation and discussion, while checking against large numbers of learning objectives can quickly become unmanageable. It also seems unlikely that the ICT resources would be so plentiful as to allow mass assessment even if it were practicable. Assessment through observation however does not necessarily mean that the practitioner has to be with the child, or children, being assessed at all times. Planning which considers the balance between independent activity, teacher participation, or group discussion may be a useful approach to take. For example, when assessing a group of young children engaged in work involving ICT:

- A practitioner could visit the group at regular intervals of time through an activity (for example, every few minutes);

- She/he could visit the group at fixed points during a task (for example, at the beginning, in the middle and at the end);

- She/he could work down a list of the children.

Practitioners may wish to consult Sharman *et al.* (1995) or similar publications for practical guidance on observing young children's learning and development and for further information on the advantages and limitations of a range of observation techniques, including written narratives, checklists, time sampling, tracking and pie/bar charts.

Organizing adult support

Most early years practitioners are involved in working with other adults in the classroom, although in England and Wales at least, the number and availability of non-teaching colleagues may be much more favourable in nursery settings than it is in reception classes. Non-teaching colleagues may include nursery nurses, special needs teachers, language support teachers, specialist classroom assistants or students as well as parent helpers and other volunteers. All these adults have a valuable contribution to make in supporting children's learning about and through ICT. Figure 15 illustrates how one reception teacher made use of other adults in the classroom to assist with work involving ICT. In some cases other adults may have particular skills and knowledge of use in teaching and learning involving ICT. In Figure 10 (p. 43), the traffic light model was constructed and wired by a volunteer helper. Similarly in Figure 14 the CCTV equipment was provided by a classroom helper who had contacts in the audio visual department of a local teacher training institution. Volunteer helpers and other adults can also assist the practitioner in promoting positive dispositions towards ICT by offering role models for children, and one of the key behaviours they can model in ICT is interest and enthusiasm.

There are a number of steps practitioners can take in order to make the most of the adult support in the nursery or classroom; the first of which is to ensure that the adults are aware of the purpose of any activity involving ICT. One way of achieving this is to adopt an inclusive approach to planning in which, while the teacher has responsibility for producing the final documentation, other members of the team are included in the discussions and generation of ideas. This was the case in both sets of examples from the nursery and reception classes used in this book. A second requirement is that adults have been properly introduced to the technology. Adults who lack confidence in their own technical ability may be reluctant to challenge children in this area for fear that they may be unable to fully support the children's learning or that the technology will malfunction. As was indicated in the earlier sections much of the ICT used in early years settings will not be particularly difficult to master, for example, operating the listening station/tape recorder. However, other resources may require the teacher to organise some form of induction, for example, learning how a new piece of software works, operating the digital camera or programming the Roamer. This is not to say that the teacher will be the trainer, indeed they may be one of the trainees, the ICT expertise may lie elsewhere in the early years team or within the wider school.

Assessing young children's developing ICT capability is yet another aspect of practice in which practitioners can benefit from deploying the skills of the whole team. Classroom observation requires attention and concentration and teachers need to consider not only those children who are being observed, but also the rest of the class particularly where non-teaching support is very limited. Failure to do this adequately could lead to constant interruptions as children request permission, mediation, instruction, advice and adjudication. As the teacher cannot be everywhere at once, the involvement of the whole team under the guidance of the teacher makes the task of focusing on groups and individuals much more manageable in terms of creating time and opportunities to observe and talk with the children. Parents and non-teaching colleagues can all play an invaluable role in monitoring and reporting on young children's achievements and progress with ICT and it is the teacher's job to act as role model and advisor in this area (Edgington 1998).

Communicating with parents

In Figure 15 the video of the reception children's karaoke concert was used during a parents' evening as a way of communicating to parents about the work the children had been doing. It proved extremely popular, with many parents eager to obtain copies; and copies of the digital photographs were also displayed in the classroom so that parents bringing their children to school could see what the children had been doing. A successful partnership with parents is often cited as a vital prerequisite for quality early years provision (Strahan 1994; Edwards and Knight 1994; QCA 2000). Teachers are continuing a learning process that has been begun by parents. The potential benefits of an effective partnership with parents are numerous. Parents can support schools and nurseries by exhibiting positive attitudes towards education. They can also become much more knowledgeable about young children's learning and the curriculum, for example being persuaded of the value of play in learning, or becoming aware that ICT can include much more than just the computer. In Figure 14, for example, the ICT work involved the use of a microphone, an amplifier, a CD player, the digital camera and the video camera. Where practitioners communicate with parents about the nature of ICT, parents will be in a better position to support their child's achievements in this area of the curriculum. The gains for the children and their teachers can include increased motivation, increased confidence, and increased knowledge, understanding and skills.

Parents' own ideas about ICT may well be based on their school or work experiences rather than on any educational training. They may draw on common sense or received notions based on the images all around them in society in which ICT is equated primarily with computers. Some parents may be highly knowledgeable and skilled users of computers and assume that investing in similar hi-tech equipment in the home is essential. Some parents may feel under pressure to purchase expensive equipment that they can ill afford. Others may feel that their own ICT knowledge and skills are limited and as a result they may feel that they are unable to support children's learning in this area. While the availability of ICT in the home is on the increase and may confer an educational advantage on those children with access to it (DfEE 2000) it is by no means universally available. The increase is unevenly spread and practitioners cannot be certain about the uses to which ICT in the home is being put.

By displaying planning and children's work in the

nursery or classroom practitioners can help parents to appreciate the breadth of ICT. Practitioners can also offer parents strategies and ideas for how they can support their child's learning in ICT in ways that do not necessarily assume access to expensive computer technology in the home. Parents could help their child to develop their awareness of, and capability with, ICT in a variety of ways including:

♦ Spending time with and showing interest in the child – drawing children's attention to the use of ICT in the home (programmable washing machines, video timers) and in the world around them (pelican crossings, bar code readers in the local library);

♦ Listening, talking to and asking questions of the child – using technical vocabulary and expressions such as *CD*, *mouse*, *programme*; explaining the relationship between the mouse and the pointer on the computer screen; reading information together from a screen; listening to taped stories and music together; stopping/pausing a video to talk about the characters or events;

♦ Developing children's practical skills – giving children the chance (with supervision where appropriate) to switch things on and off, change channels, play, rewind, fast forward and record, changing CDs, using the mouse, clicking and double clicking.

♦ Encouraging the child to find out, explore, solve problems and try out new things – seeking information using CD-ROMs or the internet (see www.naeyc.org or www.ictadvice.org.uk for guidance on using the internet);

♦ Playing with the child – using programmable or battery operated toys, computer games, musical keyboards, taping and playing back the child's own songs.

Summary

For some early years practitioners at least, ICT may conjure up intimidating images of hi-tech and high skills levels. ICT seems to be developing and changing at an increasingly rapid pace so that maintaining ICT expertise requires ongoing and continuous updating of skills. This is not easy to achieve in busy early years settings and adults who already feel under-skilled in an area may be reluctant to risk exposing what they perceive as a weakness. Paradoxically as ICT equipment becomes more technologically sophisticated it may also become more user friendly; windows environments are a good example of this. Ironically the extremely short half-life of ICT expertise could actually be a *great leveller* (Monteith 1998). As everyone is faced with the same challenge, so it is possible to enter the race to keep up to date on a more equal footing due to the lack of sequential or hierarchical knowledge necessary to become competent. Yet none of this can avoid the fact that some new technologies will require training, induction and support and it may not always be apparent where such training and support might be located.

The Role of the Practitioner in Teaching

Early years practitioners need to bear in mind that no one can realistically be expected to be an expert in everything ICT related, nor is this necessary. Partnerships of various kinds in which early years practitioners provide the pedagogical expertise necessary for work with young children, while others provide some technical *know how* and/or equipment are one way forward, provided that parity of esteem exists between those possessing early years expertise and those possessing ICT expertise. Parents, spouses, volunteers, school based ICT co-ordinators, local businesses and agencies as well as Local Education Authority personnel all constitute a valuable resource which practitioners can tap into for support. Similarly, secondary schools, local colleges and universities employ staff with ICT as well as educational skills and knowledge. They may also have access to equipment and resources not easily available to early years practitioners in the normal course of events. Where nurseries and infant schools are part of educational pyramids, secondary colleagues in other schools could be approached with a view to offering assistance. Where nurseries and schools are providing placements for students in further and higher education, training institutions may also be persuaded to get involved. Work with ICT might offer interesting projects for students training for employment in early years settings. If you do not have it, perhaps you can borrow it. If you do not know it, perhaps you know someone that does.

While much research is still to be done on good practice with ICT in the early years, practitioners can draw on their existing expertise and experience of working with young children, and use the literature on teaching and learning with ICT to guide them. To begin with, early years practitioners may find it much easier to see the relevance of and opportunities for ICT by recognising that computers are one part of a much larger whole. ICT encompasses a wide range of technologies, many of which early years practitioners are already very familiar with. Early years practitioners committed to a play based approach to learning characterised by first-hand experience and talk with peers and adults, can easily accommodate the introduction of ICT. By thinking imaginatively and creatively it is possible to move beyond the free standing computer based drill and skill programmes and begin to integrate a range of new technologies into existing provision across different areas of learning; involving both indoor and outdoor contexts. That said, the novelty of some ICT applications may generate considerable interest and excitement and this excitement could result in a short-term dip in the quality of children's play. Children need time for the novelty to wear off and for skills and knowledge to develop. It does not happen overnight and practitioners should give children the temporal space to achieve their potential.

Just as children enter nursery and reception settings at various stages of development in terms of language, behaviour, or self-image, so too they are likely to arrive with varying degrees of exposure to and familiarity with ICT. Practitioners respond to individual differences and needs in other areas of the early years curriculum, so too can provision be adapted in ICT. Practitioners routinely get involved and scaffold children's learning in the role-play area, during outdoor play, or at the writing/mark making table. The same involvement with ICT needs to take place to assist children in *showing an interest in ICT, operating equipment, performing simple functions*, and *recognizing everyday uses of ICT and incorporating ICT to support their learning* (QCA 2000: 92).

References

Alliance for Childhood (2000), 'Fools Gold: A critical Look at Computers and Childhood', Alliance for Childhood, *www.allianceforchildhood.org*

Anderson G. T. (2000), 'Computers in a Developmentally Appropriate Curriculum', *Young Children*, March: 90–3

Appleyard D. (1997), 'Switched-on kids', *Parents*, April: 56

Baker P. (1999), 'If this was the computer we could hear the lion go roar – Information and Communications Technology in Early Years Education', in Abbott L. and Moylett H. (Eds), *Early Education Transformed*, London, Falmer Press

Benjamin J. (2000), 'It makes you think', Nursery World, March: 14–5

Blenkin G. and Kelly V. (2000), 'The Concept of Infancy – A Case for Reconstruction', *Early Years*: 20, (2): 30–8

British Educational Communications and Technology Agency (2000), 'Early Years Education and ICT', BECTa, *www.becta.org.uk*

Bruce T. (1997, 2nd Edition), *Early Childhood Education*, London, Hodder & Stoughton

Caruso Davis B. and Shade D. D. (1994), 'Integrate, Don't Isolate! – Computers in the Early Childhood

Curriculum', ERIC/EECE Publications Digests, *www.ericeece.org*

Commission of the European Communities, (January, 2001), *Report from the Commission: The Concrete Future Objectives of Education Systems*, Brussels, European Commission

Cooper B. and Brna P. (2002), *'Hidden Curriculum, hidden feelings: Emotions, relationships and learning with ICT and the whole child'*, Conference Paper, British Educational Research Association

Crossley M. (2000), 'Bridging Cultures and Traditions in the Reconceptualization of Comparative and International Education', *Comparative Education*: 36, (3): 319–32

David T. (Ed) (1998), *Researching Early Childhood Education: European Perspectives*, London, Paul Chapman Publishing Ltd.

Davitt J. (Tuesday, October 17, 2000), 'Eyes on the board please', the *Guardian*, *www.guardian.co.uk/Archive*

Dawes L. (1999), *'Chalky and the interactive whiteboard: media representations of teachers and technology'*, Conference paper, British Educational Research Association

Department for Education and Children's Services South Australia (1996), *Curriculum Framework for Early Childhood Settings: Foundation Areas of Learning*, Adelaide, DECS

Department for Education and Employment (1997a), *Starting With Quality. The 1990 Report of the Committee of Inquiry into the Quality of the Educational Experience offered to 3- to 4-year-olds'*,

References

chaired by Mrs Angela Rumbold CBE MP, London, HMSO

Department for Education and Employment (1997b), *Connecting the Learning Society*, London, HMSO

Department for Education and Employment (1997c), *Excellence in Schools: A Sound Beginning, London*, HMSO

Department for Education and Employment (2000), *Survey of Schoolchildren's Use of Computers: A Report*, London, HMSO

Department of Education and Science (1989), *Design and Technology for Ages 5 to 16*, London, HMSO

Department of Education and Science (1989b), *Information Technology from 5 to 16: Curriculum Matters 15*, London, HMSO

Department of Education and Science (1992), *The education of children under five*, London, HMSO

Department for Education and Skills (2001), 'Towards Full Employment in a Modern Society', DfES, *www.dfee.gov.uk/*

Department for Trade and Industry/Department for Education and Employment (2001), 'Opportunity for all in a world of change', DTI/DfEE, *www.dti.gov.uk/*

Donaldson M. (1978), *Children's Minds*, London, Fontana Press

Early Childhood Education Forum (1998), *Quality in Diversity in Early Learning: A Framework for Early Childhood Practitioners*, London, National Children's Bureau

Edgington M. (1998, 2nd Edition), *The Nursery Teacher in Action: Teaching 3, 4 and 5-Year Olds*, London, Paul Chapman Publishing

Edgington M. (2002), *The Great Outdoors: Developing children's learning through outdoor provision*, London, The British Association for Early Childhood Education

Edwards A. and Knight P. (1994), *Effective Early Years Education: Teaching Young Children*, Buckingham, Open University Press

Elkind D. (1996), 'Young Children and Technology: A Cautionary Note', *Young Children*: 51, (6): 22–3

Freedman T. (Tuesday June 12th, 2001), 'Primary effects', the *Guardian, www.guardian.co.uk/Archive*

Grenier J. (1999), 'Screen Watch', Nursery World, March: 14–5

Haughton E. (Tuesday February 15th, 2000), 'Hurdles for screen stars', the *Guardian, www.guardian.co.uk/Archive*

Holmes R. M. (1998), *Fieldwork with children*, Thousand Oaks California, Sage Publications

Hyson M. C. (1994), *The Emotional Development of Young Children: Building an Emotion Centered Curriculum*, New York, Teachers College Press

Information Network on Education in Europe (Eurydice), (2004 Edition) 'Information and communication technology in education systems in Europe', Office for Official Publications of the European Communities, *www.eurydice.org/*

Isaacs S. (1929), *The Nursery Years*, London, Routledge Kegan Paul

Isaacs S. (1932), *The Children We Teach*, London, University of London Press

Isaacs S. (1951, Abridged Edition), *Social Development in Young Children*, London, Routledge Kegan Paul

References

Keenan T. (2002), *An Introduction to Child Development*, London, Sage Publications

Kelly K. (February 9th, 2000), 'False Promise', US News Online, *www.usnews.com/*

Kenny J. (June 8th, 2001), 'Ofsted critical of £230m training', *Times Educational Supplement*, *www.tes.co.uk/*

Kienbaum J. and Trommsdorff G. (1999), 'Social development of young children in different cultural systems', *International Journal of Early Years Education*: 7, (3): 241–48

MacNaughton G. (1997), 'Who's got the power? Rethinking gender equity strategies in early childhood', *International Journal of Early Years Education*: 5, (1): 57–66

Marsh C. (1994), 'People matter: The role of adults in providing a quality learning environment for the early years', in Abbott L. and Rodger R. (Eds), *Quality Education in the Early Years*, Buckingham, Open University Press

Mason J. and Steadman B. (1996), 'The significance of the conceptualization of childhood for promoting children's contributions to child protection policy', Australian Institute of Family Studies, *www.aifs.org.au/*

Matthews J. and Jessel J. (1993), 'Very young children and electronic paint: The beginning of drawing with traditional media and computer paintbox', *Early Years*: 13, (2): 15–22

McVeigh T. and Paton Walsh N. (Sunday September 24th, 2000), 'Computers kill pupils' creativity', *The Observer*, *www.observer.co.uk/*

Meade A. (2000), 'If you say it three times, is it true?

Critical use of research in early childhood education', *International Journal of Early Years Education*: 8, (1): 15–26

Meltz B. F. (January 10th 1998), 'Computers, software can harm emotional, social development', *Boston Globe*, *www.boston.com/globe/columns/meltz*

Merry R. (2002), 'Inside the learning mind: primary children and their learning potential', in Moyles J. and Robinson G. (Eds. 2nd Edition), *Beginning Teaching: Beginning Learning in Primary Education*, Buckingham, Open University Press

Monteith M. (1998), 'A new golden age? New technologies and learning', in Cashdan A. and Overall L. (Eds), *Teaching in Primary Schools*, London, Cassell

Moyles J., Adams S. and Musgrove A. (2002), 'SPEEL: Study of Pedagogical Effectiveness in Early Learning', DfES Research Brief No. RB363, *www.dfes.gov.uk/research/*

National Association for the Education of Young Children (1996), 'NAEYC Position Statement: Technology and Young Children – Ages Three through Eight', *Young Children*: 51, (6): 11–6

National Association for the Education of Young Children (1998) 'Early Years are Learning Years: The Internet and Young Children', NAEYC, *www.naeyc.org*

National Association of Advisers for Computers in Education & British Educational Communications and Technology Agency (2001), *Key Characteristics of Good Quality Teaching and Learning with ICT: A discussion Document*, Nottingham, NAACE/BECTa

National Curriculum Council (1990), *Curriculum Guidance 3: The Whole Curriculum*, York, NCC

References

Nutbrown C. (1996), *Respectful Educators – Capable Learners: Children's Rights and Early Education*, London, Paul Chapman

Office for Standards in Education (1995), *Information Technology: A review of Inspection Findings 1993/4*, London, Ofsted

Office for Standards in Education (2000), 'Annual Report of Her Majesty's Chief Inspector of Schools 1998–99', Ofsted, *www.official-documents.co.uk*

O'Hara M. (2000), *Teaching 3–8*, London, Continuum

Oppenheimer T. (July, 1997), 'The Computer Delusion', The Atlantic Online, *www.theatlantic.com/*

Passig D. and Levin H. (2000), 'Gender preferences for multimedia interfaces', *Journal of Computer Assisted Learning*: 16, (1): 64–71

Pierce P. L. (1994), 'Technology Integration into Early Childhood Curricula: Where We've Been, Where We Are, Where We Should Go', ERIC/EECE Publications Digests, *www.ericeece.org*

Qualifications and Curriculum Authority (1998), 'Curriculum for under-fives: Conference Report. The Review of the Desirable Outcomes for children's learning on entering compulsory education', QCA, *www.qca.org.uk/edunder5*

Qualifications and Curriculum Authority (1999), *The National Curriculum: Handbook for Primary Teachers in England. Key Stages 1 and 2*, London, QCA

Qualifications and Curriculum Authority (2000), *Curriculum Guidance for the Foundation Stage*, London, QCA

Reidy H. (1992), 'No sticky fingers, please', *Child Education*, July: 12

Revell P. (Tuesday June 12th 2001a), 'State of the nation', the *Guardian*, *www.guardian.co.uk/Archive*

Revell P. (Tuesday June 12th 2001b), 'A long way to go yet', the *Guardian*, *www.guardian.co.uk/Archive*

Sayeed Z. and Guerin E. (2000), *Early Years Play*, London, David Fulton Publishers

School Curriculum and Assessment Authority (1996), *Nursery Education: Desirable Outcomes for Children's Learning on Entering Compulsory Education*, London, SCAA

School Curriculum and Assessment Authority (1997), *Looking at Children's Learning: Desirable Outcomes for Children's Learning on Entering Compulsory Education*, London, SCAA

Sharp J., Potter J., Allen J. and Loveless A. (2000), *Primary ICT: Knowledge, Understanding and Practice*, Exeter, Learning Matters Ltd.

Sharman C., Cross W. and Vennis D. (1995), *Observing Children: A Practical Guide*, London, Cassell

Siraj-Blatchford J. and Siraj-Blatchford I. (2001), *IBM KidSmart Early Learning Programme: UK Evaluation Report – Phase 1*, London, IBM

Siraj-Blatchford J. and Siraj-Blatchford I. (2002), 'Guidance for Practitioners on Appropriate Technology Education in Early Childhood', DATEC, *www.ioe.ac.uk/cdl/datec*

Siraj-Blatchford I., Sylva K., Muttock S., Gilden R. and Bell D. (2002), 'Researching Effective Pedagogy in the Early Years', DfES Research Brief No. 356, *www.dfes.gov.uk/research/*

Smidt S. (2002, 2nd Edition), *A Guide to Early Years Practice*, London, Routledge/Falmer

References

SMSR Ltd. (June 1999), 'Review of Desirable Learning Outcomes Consultation Report', SMSR Ltd., *www.smsr.co.uk*

Strahan H. (1994), 'You feel like you belong: establishing partnership between parents and educators', in Abbott L. and Rodger R. (Eds), *Quality Education in the Early Years*, Buckingham, Open University Press

The Stevenson Report (1997), 'ICT in School Commission 1996/7', *www.ultraweb.anglia.ac.uk*

Vandevelde M. (1999), 'Planetary influences', in Abbott L. and Moylett H. (Eds), *Early Education Transformed*, London, Falmer Press

Weeks B. (2000), 'What are the most effective teaching strategies for Information Technology in the Early Years', MAPE, *www.mape.org.uk/curriculum/earlyyears/it.htm*

Wood D. (1998 2nd Edition), *How children think and learn*, Oxford, Blackwell

GRIMSBY INSTITUTE OF
LIBRARIES
FURTHER & HIGHER EDUCATION